I0825185

Praise for *The Imperfect CEO*

"*The Imperfect CEO* is a breath of fresh air in a world obsessed with shiny leadership veneers. It reminds me of a truth we lived at WD-40 Company: you don't need to be perfect—you just need to care, learn, and create a place where people can do their best work. Jim Brown shows leaders how to turn "oopses" into opportunities, build cultures where blame goes to die, and strengthen accountability in ways that actually lift people up. His stories are real, his model is practical, and his heart for people comes through on every page. If you want to lead a tribe—not just manage a team—this is the book you'll read, share, and dog-ear."

— Garry Ridge, Chairman Emeritus, WD-40 Company; *USA Today* Bestselling Author, *Any Dumb-Ass Can Do It*; and The Culture Coach

"*The Imperfect CEO* is a book for leaders who believe, like I do, that culture is the heartbeat of a healthy business. Jim Brown puts real words to the day-to-day realities we all face—building teams, handling pressure, and keeping people first while growing an organization the right way. Nothing here is theory; it's lived experience, and it shows.

As I read, I kept nodding. Jim lays out the habits that build trust and the blind spots that quietly chip away at it. This book gives leaders a clear path to creating an environment where people want to do great work and stick around. It's one I'll be sharing with my team."

— David Hopper, Board Chair, LeaderOne Financial

"After years in the C-suite, leading through complexity and transformation, I've learned this: culture isn't a 'soft' variable—it's the decisive one. In *The Imperfect CEO*, Jim Brown captures the real work of leadership with clarity and courage. He shows how humility, accountability, and trust shape performance far more than strategy decks or org charts ever will. This book isn't about polishing perfection; it's about building leaders and cultures that can actually thrive. Every CEO—and every leader who wants to be one—should read it."

— Monica Cohen, Executive Advisor and Speaker, and former Senior Executive, $24B Dairy Farmers of America

"I learned a long time ago that leadership is about how people are wired and function to achieve results in the real world. Boiled down to its essence, leadership is about making relationships and results work together—*love* and *expectations*. Too little love, and high expectations destroy any hope of sustainable results. Too little expectation, and the results never appear. This book goes straight at this dilemma of integrating and the deeper issue many CEOs face: imbalance *within themselves*. Jim has given a structure for leaders to first examine themselves and then build their organizations in alignment with how humans are designed to be fruitful. Read this book and allow it to coach you to grow and lead so everyone gets better."

– Dr. Henry Cloud, New York Times Bestselling Author, *Boundaries*; Psychologist; and Leadership Consultant

"As a university president, I see every day how culture shapes outcomes—whether in a classroom, a research lab, or an executive team. *The Imperfect CEO* names that truth with unusual clarity. Jim Brown gives leaders a framework that is both practical and deeply human, showing how trust, accountability, and shared purpose turn good intentions into real momentum. His Ascent Model resonates with what we teach our students and expect from our leadership: growth rooted in humility, clarity, and collaboration. This book will challenge leaders to rethink how they show up—and it will equip them to build cultures where people can do their best work. It's a timely guide for anyone responsible for leading people through complexity."

— Scott Green, President, University of Idaho

"Jim Brown's *The Imperfect CEO* is a masterclass in leadership for the moment—melding hard truth with generous insight and actionable guidance.

Having led communications in several Fortune 50 companies and chairing a major healthcare system board, I've seen what happens when four working generations, sweeping technology shifts, and cultural ambiguity collide in the C-suite. This book speaks to that collision zone with clarity, nuance, and urgency.

Through vivid stories, real-world examples, and a model grounded in collaborative culture, Jim gives leaders permission to wrestle honestly with the generational divides, misaligned targets, and cultural fractures that can too often sabotage high-potential organizations.

Like Jim's must-read first book on board service, *The Imperfect CEO* is grounded in a wealth of large enterprise experience but accessible enough for a startup or a church leadership team. It belongs on the desk of every leader who believes culture can propel companies—or poison them."

— Brian Besanceney, former Chief Communications Officer (Fortune 50 companies: Walmart & Boeing); Chair, Board of Orlando Health, Inc.

"Healthy, high-performing organizations aren't commanded by hierarchy but cultivated by humility. In *The Imperfect CEO*, Jim shows how human-centred leadership drives the relationships and results the world needs."

— Allison Alley, President and CEO, World Vision Canada

"In every organization I've led, one truth has been constant: culture determines whether strategy ever sees daylight. *The Imperfect CEO* gets to the heart of that reality. Jim Brown captures the subtle choices leaders face every day. They either build trust or quietly erode it. His blend of story, insight, and practical guidance makes complex issues feel doable, even for teams under pressure. I especially appreciated how he helps leaders stay human without losing effectiveness. This book is a timely reminder that imperfect leaders, when self-aware and grounded, can create extraordinary environments for people to thrive."

— Edna Lopez, former Senior Executive, Farelogix and Amadeus

"*The Imperfect CEO* speaks directly to the leadership realities I see every day in churches and other Christian-led organizations. Jim Brown masterfully uses the ancient art of story-telling to give leaders a clear, grace-filled pathway for building healthy teams—rooted in trust, clarity, and accountability. What struck me most is how actionable his insights are. They help leaders navigate conflict, align around mission, and create cultures where people flourish and ministries thrive. This book doesn't shy away from the tough stuff; it meets leaders right where they are and gives them tools that work in real life. I recommend it to every faith-based leader who wants to strengthen their organization's culture, maximize their impact, and better reflect Christ to the world."

— Jay Bransford, CEO, Best Christian Workplaces

"*The Imperfect CEO* captures the tension many of us feel as leaders who care deeply about people and performance. I saw myself in these pages—especially in the moments where valuing people was mistaken for inattention to business. What I appreciated most was the practicality of the insights; these are ideas you can put to the test in the here and now. This book shows why collaboration and culture aren't soft—they're the backbone of lasting success."

— Shari Sekel, CEO, PenFinancial Credit Union

"In my work with students and leaders across generations, I see a common thread: people want meaning, clarity, and a culture they can trust. *The Imperfect CEO* captures that reality better than any leadership book I've read. Jim Brown moves past stereotypes about Millennials, Gen Z, or Boomers and gets to the heart of what actually drives performance—shared purpose, honest communication, respectful inclusion, and leaders who own the environment they create. The stories are real, the framework is practical, and the cultural insights are spot on, If you're leading a team in today's fractured workplace, this book will help you build a culture where people can thrive together."

— Jeff LeBlanc, Lecturer, Management, Bentley University,
and Author, *Engaged Empathy Leadership*

"In industries defined by disruption and rapid reinvention, such as the travel industry, leaders need more than technical skill—they need a way to make sense of complexity while keeping their teams grounded. *The Imperfect CEO* offers exactly that. Jim Brown gives leaders a practical framework for navigating growth, tension, and change without losing their people along the way. His stories ring true for anyone who has led through expansion, restructuring, or shifting market realities. What impressed me most is how usable the Ascent Model is—clear, memorable, and immediately applicable. For leaders who want to elevate performance while strengthening trust, this book provides a roadmap that actually works."

— Ellen L. Keszler, former Executive Officer,
American Airlines, Sabre, and Travelocity

"*The Imperfect CEO* is a timely and compelling book. Company culture has been a sleeper issue for too long, but Jim Brown shines a light on it with clarity and urgency. Both management teams and boards now have a practical tool to see where they are and how to get where they need to be.

Having invested in and served on the boards of more than 20 early-stage companies, I only wish this accessible model had been available for every one of them. It would have helped prevent the all-too-common distractions that arise when growth outpaces attention to culture."

—Terrell Jones, Founder, Travelocity; Founding
Chairman, KAYAK; and Chairman, Amgine.ai

"*The Imperfect CEO* does for leadership what *The Imperfect Board Member* did for governance. Jim Brown lays out a clear pathway that guides leaders at any level to lead their teams to sustained fruitfulness, drawing out their team members' creativity and building the workplace environment that will keep them engaged and flourishing. As a senior leader, I found the book inspirational, affirming, and helpful."

— John Pellowe, CEO, Canadian Centre for Christian Charities

"In a fast-moving tech company, culture is everything. Jim Brown's principles have helped our team lead with greater clarity and alignment. *The Imperfect CEO* distills those lessons brilliantly. Every leader should read it."

— Greg Apple, CEO, Amgine.ai

Early in my career at Procter & Gamble I learned that performance is driven not just by process, but by the beliefs, behaviors, and culture of the team behind it. In *The Imperfect CEO*, Jim Brown takes that truth seriously and gives it a home in leadership practice. He doesn't shy away from the messy reality of being a real person in charge, yet he shows how that honesty becomes a source of organizational health. If you're a leader who knows the numbers matter, but you also know it's the culture that really moves them, this book will change how you lead.

— Larry Siff, CEO, Neptune Advisors and C-Level Community

"As someone who has spent decades strengthening pastors, coaching church leaders, and serving ministries across the nation, I don't often read a leadership book that feels this close to real life. *The Imperfect CEO* read like someone had been walking beside me through the highs, the heartbreaks, and the holy weight of leading God's people. Jim Brown names what many of us experience but rarely articulate—and he does it with insight that sticks. This book will steady leaders who feel stretched and remind them what healthy, faith-filled leadership can actually look like."

— Adam Durso, President, Leading Leaders Collective

"*The Imperfect CEO* is a thoughtful and timely contribution to the leadership conversation. Jim Brown captures the lived reality of guiding people through complexity and change, and he does it with clarity and heart. His framework helps leaders foster environments where trust grows, purpose strengthens, and teams move forward together. This book will serve anyone committed to leading with integrity and genuine care."

— Marc Jerry, President, Renison University College, University of Waterloo

"Having known Jim Brown for over 20 years, I can attest that his wisdom and authenticity shine through every page of *The Imperfect CEO.* Jim's blend of honest storytelling and practical frameworks offers leaders a clear path to building healthier, more human organizations. His focus on trust, vulnerability, and growth is both timely and transformative. This book is a must-read for anyone seeking to lead with heart and real impact."

– Santiago "Jimmy" Mellado, President and Chief Executive Officer, Compassion International

THE IMPERFECT CEO

Also by Jim Brown

The Imperfect Board Member:
Discovering the Seven Disciplines of Governance Excellence

THE IMPERFECT CEO

Making the Climb to Organizational Health

JIM BROWN

Matt Holt Books
An Imprint of BenBella Books, Inc.
Dallas, TX

This book is designed to provide accurate and authoritative information about organizational culture. Neither the author nor the publisher is engaged in rendering legal, accounting, or other professional services by publishing this book. If any such assistance is required, the services of qualified professionals should be sought. The author and publisher will not be responsible for any liability, loss, or risk incurred as a result of the use and application of any information contained in this book.

Matt Holt is an imprint of BenBella Books, Inc.
8080 N. Central Expressway
Suite 1700
Dallas, TX 75206
benbellabooks.com
Send feedback to feedback@benbellabooks.com

BenBella and *Matt Holt* are federally registered trademarks.

Printed in the United States of America
10 9 8 7 6 5 4 3 2 1

Library of Congress Control Number: 2025046897
ISBN 9781637749029 (hardcover)
ISBN 9781637749036 (electronic)

Copyediting by Scott Calamar
Proofreading by Lisa Story and Ashley Casteel
Indexing by Debra Bowman
Text design and composition by PerfecType, Nashville, TN
Cover design by Jason Arias
Cover image © Shutterstock / Penpitcha Pensiri
Printed by Lake Book Manufacturing

CONTENTS

Part II: The Model

FOREWORD
by Stephen M. R. Covey

The Imperfect CEO beautifully delivers something rare in leadership literature: a deeply honest, highly practical, and distinctively human roadmap for leading organizations through a changing, shifting, disruptive world. And it's done with both humility and courage.

The combination of both a story and a teaching model is masterfully done. You'll be drawn in by the fable—a vivid and relatable narrative that holds up a mirror to modern leadership—and then grounded in a model that gives you a clear, practical path forward. As with all of Jim Brown's work, this is not mere theory. Instead, it's intensely practical and actionable, even transformational.

The great thing is that you don't need to be a CEO to benefit from this book! *Any* leader can benefit. You just need to be willing to grow. You just need to be open to the idea that your leadership story isn't finished, and that your best contribution may lie not in being the perfect leader, but in being the *learning* one.

But before we talk about the book, let me tell you a little more about the person behind it.

The Person

I first met Jim after a conference in Canada where I had presented on my book, *The Speed of Trust*, and he had presented on his earlier wonderful book, *The Imperfect Board Member*. We took the time then to start to get to genuinely know each other, which ignited a close friendship that's spanned nearly two decades. *The Imperfect Board Member* has had staying power during this time, not only because of the insights Jim provides but also because he lives the enduring principles he writes about.

Jim's a trusted consultant to boards of directors, CEOs, and senior leadership teams across industries and countries. He's taught and coached hundreds of leaders. And he's built and refined a unique and effective framework for creating "organizational health," not as a buzzword but rather as a measurable, livable reality.

During that time, I've come to know Jim well enough to say, with great confidence, that he is one of the most insightful, wise, and caring people I have ever met. He's a convincingly good human being.

And his leadership voice is equally strong, clear, and compelling.

What's always stood out to me most magnificently about Jim is his character, which is manifest in the way he leads, coaches, and teaches. Among many talents, he has a gift for making complex things simple. He is simultaneously deeply insightful while also being immensely practical. He teaches principles without arrogance, and he's relevant without the ego.

On top of that, he both leads and writes from a starting place of trust.

And now, with *The Imperfect CEO*, Jim offers that same grounded wisdom to leaders at every level who are willing to embrace something more powerful than perfection: progress.

The Premise

This remarkable book starts with a premise that's both sobering and hopeful: Many CEOs today are feeling increasingly out of sync with their own people and culture, and they don't quite know why. What used to work in the past doesn't seem to work as well anymore.

Jim takes us right into that dynamic through a compelling story. It's a leadership fable that reads like real life. Because it is real life. David Slater, the protagonist, is not a caricature. He's not a villain. He's a capable, accomplished, well-intentioned CEO who finds himself increasingly at odds with his team, his culture, and even his own instincts. Through his eyes, as well as through the voices of his executive team, we see the clash between outdated leadership paradigms and today's vital need for something more.

Those moments of reckoning when a leader is willing to confront their own blind spots is where this book shines. It doesn't shame. It doesn't blame. It simply invites the reader to ask an honest question: *What if there's a better way to lead?*

And there is.

This narrative brings vividly to life the very shift I explore in my own work, *Trust & Inspire*, around the journey for leaders and organizations to move from "Command & Control" to "Trust & Inspire." Jim dramatizes this shift in story. And the result is extraordinary.

In the past, command and control was seen as a strength. Now, it's becoming increasingly irrelevant, even a liability.

In the past, leadership was about being the smartest person in the room. Now, it's about seeing, communicating, developing, and unleashing the greatness of others.

In the past, success meant managing people. Now, it requires *trusting* and *inspiring* them.

The Framework

The fable unfolds alongside a simple yet powerful framework: the OrgHealth Ascent Model. This model identifies four essential components of a healthy, high-functioning organization:

1. **Collaborative Culture**—where silos come down, voices are heard, and the team works together for the good of the whole.
2. **Leadership Accountability**—where those in charge model the values and behaviors they expect from others.
3. **Strategic Momentum**—where there's not just a plan but a living, breathing strategy that's aligned, communicated, and advancing.
4. **Talent Magnetism**—where people don't just stay, they thrive in such a way that others want to join them too.

Each of these elements is essential. Lacking any one of them will impact organizational health. And all of them are dramatically enhanced by one thing: trust.

Trust is not merely a soft, nice-to-have social virtue. Rather, it's a hard-edged economic driver and performance multiplier. It's the one thing that changes everything. And in *The Imperfect CEO*,

Jim shows exactly how trust (or the absence of it) shows up in every part of organizational life, from culture and communication to performance and purpose.

In short, if you want organizational health, you have to focus on all four elements of the Ascent Model. That's what this book helps you do. And all four elements work dramatically better when built on a foundation of trust.

The Heart

What makes *The Imperfect CEO* especially powerful is its emotional and relational honesty. The story doesn't sugarcoat the tensions that show up in leadership teams: the miscommunications, the assumptions, the tone-deaf moments, the eroding trust. You'll find yourself wincing at some of the exchanges because they're so familiar. But you'll also find yourself inspired by the breakthroughs, especially the courage of a leader to say, "I don't know how to fix this, but I know I need to."

That moment of vulnerability is the turning point.

It's also the key to everything.

The reality is that the old way of leading is no longer sufficient for the challenges and expectations of our time. Today's workforce doesn't want to be managed, but they do want to be led. And they especially want to be led by someone they can trust. Someone real.

Real doesn't mean flawless. Real means *honest. Authentic. Learning. Evolving.*

That's why I believe this book matters. Because it shows, through story and structure, how leadership is no longer about perfection but rather about *connection*. It's about inspiration and collaboration. And it's about modeling the behavior you'd like to see, trusting those you lead, and inspiring others by connecting with people and connecting to purpose. This is doing the inner work to become the kind of leader others want to follow.

The Invitation

So, here's my invitation to you as a reader: Don't just read this book. Work with it. Apply it. Test it.

Jim has brilliantly structured the book to be more than a story but also a *coaching experience*. At the end of key chapters, you'll find "Coaching Highlights" with questions, prompts, and practical tools you can use immediately to reflect, adapt, and apply. These are not theoretical exercises; they are real-world practices designed to help you lead better, starting now.

Being "imperfect" is not an indictment, but rather a vital and necessary condition. Because the imperfect leader who listens, learns, and leads with trust and purpose is the one who will build the healthiest organizations. As well as the most enduring legacies.

Jim has given us a gift by showing us the way. And it comes at the right time.

The world is desperately in need of leaders who are less interested in looking good and more interested in doing good. Who are less interested in being right and more interested in doing what is right. Who are willing to admit what they don't know and eager to learn what they should. Who understand that health matters: not just physical health but also cultural, relational, and organizational health.

That kind of leadership begins not with perfect mastery, but rather with genuine honesty. It requires both humility and courage simultaneously, to go along with authenticity and vulnerability. And it is elevated by a combination of empathy and performance.

The Imperfect CEO is a guide to that kind of leadership.

So, take this book seriously. Let it challenge you. Let it coach you. Let it change the way you show up as a leader.

Because when you lead from a place of trust, humility, and courage, your imperfection won't hold you back.

It will *open you up*. To growth. To connection. To impact. To inspiration. To what's possible.

And that's the kind of leadership we need now more than ever.

Stephen M. R. Covey
The New York Times and #1 *Wall Street Journal* best-selling author of *The Speed of Trust* and *Trust & Inspire*

INTRODUCTION

At the age of 18, I got a job in a factory. I liked it. I was thankful for full-time employment and a decent wage. School had been a pain, so this was a welcome change. Having grown up on a farm, I was used to work being a normal part of life. There was nothing that the job demanded that was unreasonable to me. But I quickly discovered this was not the case for most of my coworkers. I'm a morning person. Punching the clock at 7:45 AM to start each day was no problem. I was awake and positive. I'd say good morning to the people around me in line. The automatic response from most of them was *f*** off.* Mondays were especially hard for people because they seemed to be repeatedly recovering from a wild party. People constantly told me they hated their job. When I asked why they didn't quit, they'd say they didn't know what else they'd do, or they had a mortgage and couldn't risk it. Even men and women in their thirties literally felt trapped. So they medicated themselves on weekends with drugs and alcohol. I was shocked to eventually learn that this was widespread. The idea that a large proportion of the population was spending most of their waking hours in jobs they detested horrified me. And after a few years of enduring the constant negativity, I decided to take my own advice. I quit my job and went back to school. I had a mission.

Imagine our world where almost everyone loves the work they do. That would be a stark contrast to the current reality. Some statistics show only half of the workforce likes their jobs.* Other reports suggest even lower numbers.

I've spent my life working to improve this situation. Wonderfully, it's absolutely possible. Leaders have the opportunity to transform the work experience so that their employees do love their jobs. We know this because there are plenty of examples where it's already true.

The purpose of this book is to help you join the growing force of people committed to making work a fulfilling part of life rather than a regrettable burden. You can do it for yourself and for the people working with you.

This book's composed of two sections. The first is a fable about a leader discovering how unhealthy his company is and working with his team to develop a way to understand what's wrong and what to do about it. The second section is our explanation of the model that's unfolded in the story. I'm going to spill the beans right away . . . There are four indicators of an organization being healthy. They're not complicated. Curiously, though, they're not obvious to most people. And that's a pity, because every company can quickly improve when we become aware and determined to work on these. I encourage you to be mindful of these indicators as you read the story. Very briefly, they are:

---

* Luona Lin, Juliana Horowitz, and Richard Fry, "Most Americans Feel Good About Their Job Security but Not Their Pay," Pew Research Center, December 10, 2024, https://www.pewresearch.org/social-trends/2024/12/10/most-americans-feel-good-about-their-job-security-but-not-their-pay/.

Collaborative Culture—Everyone works together to make the whole company better.

Leadership Accountability—The people leading exemplify the core values and strategic focus of the company.

Strategic Momentum—A plan to succeed is well communicated, and the company has implemented it effectively for several years.

Talent Magnetism—The company's culture and success attract skilled workers consistently.

Collaborative Culture	Leadership Accountability	Strategic Momentum	Talent Magnetism

It's completely reasonable that you may have read that list and think it's no big deal. Except it is a big deal! Building healthy organizations where people can love their jobs transforms lives and businesses and families. This book explains how.

Be warned: Parts of the fable mirror real-life situations that can be uncomfortable. You'll see moments that expose unfairness, inefficiency, and poor leadership—things that should never be ignored but too often are.

It's frustrating that so many leadership teams and boards of companies are mostly made up of men. Women are more than capable. It's frustrating that many of the people most trusted with leadership are older white guys when there's so much untapped wisdom in younger men, women, and people of other racial and ethnic heritages. It's irritating that so many people in charge have outdated views and biases that ignore reason and impede progress. It's infuriating how often people with power seem to minimize the contributions that the average workers bring or the challenges they have to overcome.

If you find yourself chafing at any of these types of scenarios in the story, be the better leader and ask yourself what you can do this week to tackle a similar problem in your real world. How would you challenge the wrong thinking or offer an enlightened understanding? Who can you encourage to keep up the fight for what is right and good?

We're actually hoping you have reactions as you're reading the story. Like wincing a little as you recognize a character behaving poorly and realizing you've done something similar yourself. Or your eyes might widen as you read about someone's reaction to something you thought was harmless. To help you process some of the issues and attitudes, we've added Coaching Highlights that give you some questions to consider and even link to some tools you might use to increase your self-awareness and skills. The lightbulb icon signals where these highlights are triggered. You'll find the extra insights at the end of the chapter where you see each icon. You can try many of the related exercises online at OrgHealthTeam.com/exercises.chapter-x, where *x* is the chapter number. Go back and scan the Contents to see the Highlight topics listed in bold text.

The fact that you're reading this book indicates you're the kind of leader who wants to grow. You're the type of person who recognizes that there's more to learn and you have to take action to make that happen. I'm praying you join me in applying energy and attention to make the world better by building healthy organizations!

> Never doubt that a small group of thoughtful, committed citizens can change the world; indeed, it's the only thing that ever has.
>
> —Margaret Mead

PART I
The Fable

CHAPTER 1

Believing the Best

Murray Webster settled into his Adirondack chair and gazed across the lake as the evening sun reflected off the water. What a life! Now in his early sixties, he enjoyed the fruit of his efforts as a seasoned investor. He had been very fortunate, sure, but his early luck had afforded him the luxury of learning from mistakes. As the CEO of an electronics company, he had been talked into joining the board of a technology venture before it went public. In five short years, it had mushroomed into a darling company in Silicon Valley. Simultaneously, another company whose board he was on had similar explosive growth. Two IPOs with exponential returns caused his financial condition to move from enviable to astonishing.

Unsurprisingly, any young tech founder that could find Murray's contact information tried to convince him that their startup was the perfect place for a slice of his surplus. And Murray had chosen a bunch that sounded promising. He was stunned by how quickly great ideas faltered—and how unapologetically founders returned to ask for more cash, claiming it would make all the difference and turn his seed money into a payoff. He had soon decided that a different approach would be wise. He became an active investor, insisting that a condition of funding any business was that he be made a member of the board. There was no resistance. Frankly, his reputation as an early board member on two companies that had reached unicorn status caused founders to view him as a startup wunderkind.

In the 20 years that followed, Murray had been involved with 26 companies and had successfully exited 11 of them. His high success ratio was a product of some high-cost learning. In a nutshell, his criteria for selecting startups that warranted his time and money had evolved to three essentials: They must face a huge market, offer remarkable technology, and be led by amazing people.

One of the amazing people he had invested in was David Slater. Murray met him 14 years earlier when a board he served on had realized their CEO founder was no longer up to the task. The search firm had offered Slater as a promising candidate, and the board's diligent review confirmed that this young man had the moxie their company needed. Slater had recently exited a business he had started almost seven years earlier, so he had a track record of leading from startup to public listing. They hired him on, and he stayed consistently courageous and unshakably open as he led that company to huge success.

David is the kind of leader Murray could believe in. So he jumped on board the next venture with him too. When David pitched his vision to build a business coupling new battery technology with AI to disrupt how electric vehicles maximize battery power for each driver, Murray could not resist.

Now he could just coast along. It seemed that everything was great. But things are not always as they seem.

CHAPTER 2
Trouble at the Top

David sat with his elbows on his desk and his head in his hands. For the third time in as many weeks, a key person had not come to work, and an important meeting had been scuttled. What in the world was going on? It used to be that people took their jobs seriously. Now it felt like people stayed home for a mild cough—or took mental health days after a bad night's sleep.

For the past four years, David had been leading EVaant,* a company focused on radically improving power use in electric vehicles. They were growing, but lately things just felt wrong.

His first venture, CommuniTrek, had been a huge success. Wise input had enabled him to overcome some difficulties with his board of directors and ultimately take the technology company public. Six years after that, he had exited with enough to retire

---

* The company name is pronounced *"EE-vaant," a play on the word avant-garde—suggesting forward-thinking, boundary-pushing leadership.*

but way more time and energy than he knew what to do with. He was relieved when a headhunter called about six months later and pitched him a spot as CEO of another tech company whose founder had become overwhelmed. The nine years he spent there allowed him to grow the staff to almost 400, progress through series A and series B funding rounds, and conclude gloriously when a global competitor negotiated the purchase of the business. A condition of the deal was that one of the executives of the acquiring company would become the CEO, so David left with a substantial severance package.

His impression was that the people he led loved him. Certainly, there were scores of previous team members and early staff who enjoyed a very prosperous lifestyle because of stock options he granted them.

Two big wins. He had presumed it was third time lucky. But he wasn't so sure anymore.

CHAPTER 3

Team Trials

The executive leadership team (ELT) was made up of six people. The company's website said:

David Slater—Chief Executive Officer
Bill Mercer—Chief Financial Officer
Rebecca Watson—Chief Operating Officer
Jorge Manriquez—Chief Revenue Officer
Marlon Williams—Chief Technology Officer
Carmen Hernandez—Chief People Officer

They met every Thursday at 10 AM. David believed weekly meetings kept everyone aligned—though in practice, he usually spent half the time outlining his own thoughts.

Today's meeting was coming to an end, he thought, when Rebecca, the COO, reacted to what he had just said. "Wait, I already told you we wouldn't get that finished on time because two of the key people took some time off for mental health." David did not even look at her. He just blurted, "For pity's sake, why don't people just suck it up and get the work done?"

Nobody spoke. Bill squeezed his lips together and nodded lightly. As CFO, he was vividly aware of how many workdays were lost to mental health claims. Tentatively, Carmen reacted. "You do realize people have a legal right to take time to recover from mental strain. That isn't irresponsibility; it's self-care."

"Well, in my day, that was not an option," David groaned. "What is so hard that people need time to recover?"

"Actually, Angelo's in a tough spot. His nine-year-old son is quite sick with leukemia. And then last week his mother passed away." Rebecca stated the facts with a tone of defensiveness.

"Oh," David huffed. "I didn't know that. You know what they say, the leader's always the last to be told."

"And sometimes it seems the leader's the last to ask," Carmen said curtly. "Why not assume that people have legitimate reasons for the choices they make?"

"Well, let's get back to our priorities," David announced, standing. "We've got a lot on our plates." The group of six filed out of the boardroom and briskly went in various directions. David walked side by side with Bill to their adjacent offices. "The women seem extra emotional today," Bill commented with a glance toward Carmen and Rebecca. "Mm-hmm," David mumbled as he headed to his desk.

▶ COACHING HIGHLIGHT

What went through your mind as you read David's reaction to some people being away from work for mental health recovery? How did you feel about it when you read

Carmen's perspective? Taking some time to process your reactions will help you grow as a leader.

Coaching Questions

1. Recall recent meetings you attended with your team. What impact do you believe your words and tone had on your team's engagement?
2. If you were in your team members' shoes, how would you feel about the company culture under your leadership?
3. What assumptions do you make about your team members' needs and motivations?
4. How do you show your team that you care about them beyond their output?
5. How do you think your leadership style has evolved since you first began influencing others at work?

Exercises

1. Read "Gen Z Isn't Quiet Quitting. They're Rejecting Outdated Leadership" in *Fast Company*. Author Jeff Leblanc outlines some expectations that Gen Z has about their workplace: psychological safety, transparency, fairness. Are those priorities for you? Are you working to ensure they become norms in your company?
2. Empathy peer practice: Sit together and randomly select a peer to answer one of the following questions. Before the chosen peer responds, invite others to share their assumptions about what they think the person might say. After the peer answers, compare these assumptions with their actual response, and discuss as a group what surprised you, what

you learned about each other, and how this reflection challenges or shifts your understanding. Continue random selection until everyone answers the same question. Highlight moments where perceptions differed from reality and how this deepened empathy within the team.

a. What invisible barrier do you face daily that others might underestimate? (Focuses on unspoken challenges, encouraging deeper reflection on systemic or personal obstacles.)
b. If you had to advocate for your most critical unmet need, what would it be, and why? (Builds awareness/understanding of priorities and gaps in support, encouraging actionable empathy.)
c. What unique strength do you possess that is undervalued? (Highlights self-perception versus external perception—and reveals hidden potential.)

Find all our resources for this Coaching Highlight at OrgHealthTeam.com/exercises/chapter-3. ◀

CHAPTER 4

The Comfort of Trees

Carmen Hernandez always thought she would grow up and work with plants. Her father ran a lawn care business, and she absorbed all he could tell her about grass and weeds and shrubs and trees. She studied the diseases they encountered in the properties they managed. She learned what varieties of grasses would grow best depending on moisture and shade and soil types. She found the smell of fresh-cut grass comforting.

But plant focus turned to people focus as she finished her teens, and she started college near her home in Carson, California. Now she was a 38-year-old chief people officer at a technology company. Her parents were exceedingly proud. She was, too, though she never said that to anyone.

That was on her good days. Some days she wondered why in the world she subjected herself to the misery of corporate life. Over a hundred people work at the company. Too many feel like cogs

in a wheel. They have a chance to brighten the world's future with innovations in EV efficiency and battery longevity. If only everyone could see the purpose their work offered.

She had worked with the CFO three years earlier to build a financial case for maximizing flexible work options for employees with up to four days per week remote. He was resistant at first, but some of her peers in the professional HR network had shared some well-documented research that demonstrated the value of increased engagement and retention of workers, especially in the demographics that EVaant employed. Bill became an advocate for the policy change. Carmen realized the ELT would not have been convinced without his help.

Needing some space, Carmen had driven to a grove of trees not too far from the office. Walking in the tranquility. Breathing in the oxygenated air enriched by the trees' photosynthesis. Feeling the peace and stillness. All of this refreshed her soul.

"Our people are good," she spoke aloud, but to herself. "It's the way the world works that sometimes brings out the worst in them." She shook her head as she thought of examples that disappointed her. Like managers who complained that when the people are working remote, it's impossible to make sure they are really doing their job. Like the woman who felt embarrassed that she needed time off to be with her daughter while her daughter was in the hospital. Like when David goes on about the stock options they are all getting on the ELT. "He just doesn't understand that money isn't the most important thing. He fails to grasp that we each need to be valued even more than we need to get paid." She scuffed the ground as she walked, frustration simmering beneath the surface.

The old pattern of work that treated employees like disposable supplies in an assembly process was so frustrating to her. "Why don't leaders see that people are the most amazing and valuable things in the world? What do I need to do to get that through their heads!" She stopped and stared up at the foliage. Glimpses of sunlight sparkled throughout. She edged closer to a tree and reached out to its steady strength. "Why can't more leaders be like you?"

CHAPTER 5
Staccato Stresses

Staring out the window, but looking at nothing, David was going over the same questions that had been repeating in his mind. *Why can't people just give me the benefit of the doubt? They know me. I'm doing everything I can to help them win. Everything. Everything to help everyone win.* He shook his head. *But they expect me to change. I'm trying, but I've got 40 years of being this way. And it's worked fine up to now. Why am I the one who has to change?*

His phone buzzed on his desk. A text message signaled that Bill needed to talk to him ahead of the board meeting.

▲▼▲

"Wait, did I just hear you say you have a bunch of open positions?" Dennis asked. The EVaant board was about 20 minutes into a video call and David had been giving commentary on his CEO update. "Maybe I missed it before, but this is the first I remember hearing you're having trouble finding people to work." Dennis Hinton was an independent board member added after the series A funding round.

"Oh, this has been a grind for a long time. It's happening everywhere. I'm surprised you haven't heard about this trend." David winced a tiny bit as his last statement registered in his own mind. Dennis might hear that as a criticism, he realized.

"David, I'm well aware of the difficulty many companies are having to attract and retain good people. I'm also aware that this is not universal. Somehow, I had the impression our company was in the sweet spot of winning in the war for talent. I guess I assumed you'd be keeping us updated on personnel issues like turnover and hiring if there were any problems."

Another board member said something that provoked everyone to move on in their agenda. But Dennis remained unsettled.

▲▼▲

The ELT was seated in the boardroom, listening as David gave some commentary on the monthly financial update. They had all agreed to delay their meeting from morning to afternoon so that the short-notice board meeting could be accommodated. Marlon pointed at a line on his report and asked, "Is this budget overrun because of that monitoring software we decided to get?" David nodded and went on.

Carmen interjected. "What are we monitoring? I don't remember talking about anything that was going to put us over budget."

"It'll probably end up saving us money in the long run," David said. "With so many people working different hours and remotely, it's impossible to supervise them. Marlon did a bit of research and found a system that tracks how people are using our computers and whether they're actually doing work." Bill jumped in, adding, "I did some reviewing on it, too, and I agree that this will let us get a window into how people are using their time."

No one missed that Carmen's eyes closed and head drooped. "Why the drama, Carmen?" David asked with a tone of irritation. She raised her head, eyes moving from face to face around the table. "You guys do read social media, don't you? Surely you've noticed posts about this over the past few years. I hope you follow people like Adam Grant and get insights about psychology in the workplace." Blank expressions were returned. "Come on! There are now dozens of studies that show workers feel distrusted and violated when electronic monitoring is done. It reduces their job satisfaction. And there's no evidence that performance improves.* It's only negative, as far as I can see."

"That makes no sense," Bill reacted. "When people realize they're being watched, they have to be more intentional to do their work. That's human nature, right?" Some others seemed to agree, but with uncertainty. "We could do some tests and confirm this," Marlon suggested.

"*Por el amor de Dios,* can't we trust the mountain of research and spare ourselves the misery this will bring?" Carmen stood slowly. "With all this group's preoccupation on cutting costs, I would have thought you'd look more carefully into whether this extra expense—over our budget—was worthwhile. I would have thought you'd ask

* Daniel M. Ravid, Jerod C. White, David L. Tomczak, Ahleah F. Miles, and Tara S. Behrend, "A Meta-Analysis of the Effects of Electronic Performance Monitoring on Work Outcomes," *Personnel Psychology* 75, no. 2 (2022): 251–288, https://doi.org/10.1111/peps.12514.

everyone around this table if they have any input before you spent the money." She turned to the door and left the room.

The remaining five looked at each other sheepishly. "I guess we'll end there," David said. People drifted out of the meeting room without a word.

▲▼▲

It was just after seven o'clock that evening when David arrived home and entered the kitchen through the garage door. "Hi, hon," he said brightly, spotting Nancy curled up on the bay window seat, the evening sun scattering light across the room. Her reply was barely audible.

"Hey," David said, his tone turning soft. "What's happening?"

Nancy rose and stepped into her husband's embrace. "I'm worried about Daniel. He was here most of the day—Simon and Ramona's sitter called in sick. It was really hard. I just wish I knew how to reach him. Even with all the research I've done about neurodivergent kids,* I'm failing."

David stiffened. "*You're* failing? He's nine, and he still can't write the letters of the alphabet." David snorted. Nancy snapped backward from him. "I can see that makes you angry. I'm angry too. The difference is that you're angry at Daniel, and I'm angry at myself. I'm so upset that I haven't been able to find a way to help him learn. I'm angry at his schoolteachers because they're supposed to be the experts, but they haven't helped him. I'm angry at the education system because everyone in it just shakes their head and

---

* "Neurodivergent" is a nonmedical term to describe people whose brain differences affect how their brain works, according to the Cleveland Clinic.

says they don't know what to do. I'm even a bit angry at Simon and Ramona for not being desperate enough to kick down doors and insist that they get their son the help that's required."

Nancy raised her eyes and looked directly at David. "I'm angry at you. You've always been my door-kicker-downer. But you haven't even tried to fight for our amazing grandson. He deserves a path that lets him shine." Her words had become sobs. David cautiously took her in his arms again.

▸ COACHING HIGHLIGHT

As you reflect on the boardroom discussion surrounding the monitoring software, consider the tension between ensuring productivity and maintaining trust. David's irritation with Carmen's concerns raises questions about leadership dynamics and employee well-being. How do you feel about the differing perspectives on monitoring? Taking a moment to process these reactions can lead to deeper insights into your leadership approach.

Coaching Questions

1. How do you balance the need for oversight with fostering trust among your team members?
2. When was the last time you solicited feedback from your team on decisions that affect their work environment? What was the outcome?
3. Reflect on a situation where you had to make a tough decision. How did you ensure that all voices were heard?
4. What strategies do you employ to create a culture of psychological safety in your team?

5. How do you communicate the rationale behind significant changes, like budget adjustments or new tools, to your team?

Exercises

1. Explore the article "How Employee Tracking Hurts Morale and Productivity" in *Worklytics*. Consider how the findings relate to your own team dynamics and how you might adjust your approach.
2. Conduct a team survey to gauge their feelings about monitoring and performance expectations. See our sample on our website. Use the results to inform your decision-making process and improve team engagement.
3. Role-Playing: Pair up with a colleague to practice how to respond to concerns about monitoring in a constructive and empathetic manner. This can help you prepare for real-life discussions.

Find all our resources for this Coaching Highlight at OrgHealthTeam.com/exercises.chapter-5. ◀

CHAPTER 6
Under the Surface

Patterns and routines were tools that David had long integrated into his life. Early to bed, early to rise. Work before play. Eat the frog.* These were default behaviors that he no longer consciously evaluated. And it seemed there were dozens more that unfortunately caused problems for some people. He had been chewing on this uncomfortable notion for some time. Carmen had mentioned that a factor to consider is the different responses people have depending on their generation. So he had googled and learned that he and Bill and Jorge were Gen X, their ages being 57, 56, and 53. Meanwhile, the other three were all millennials,

* Mark Twain is commonly credited with saying: "If it's your job to eat a frog, it's best to do it first thing in the morning. And if it's your job to eat two frogs, it's best to eat the biggest one first."

Carmen being just 38, Marlon 42, and Rebecca 44. *What does all that mean?* he wondered.

Carmen knocked lightly on the open door and walked in to sit across from David's desk. "Feels like I just got called to the principal's office," she said, sinking into the seat with a wry smile. "Did I cross a line in our meeting yesterday morning?"

"No." David was thinking about whether the fact that she was a millennial was impacting her reaction. But he abandoned the thought, admitting he did not understand that enough. "From how you and Rebecca reacted, I'm guessing *I* crossed a line. Help me understand."

His eyes gave Carmen confidence that his question was earnest.

"Well," Carmen began, "you've maybe heard the maxim 'If you want to go fast, go alone. If you want to go far, go together.' You're preprogrammed to go fast. You tend to appreciate people who can keep up with you." David nodded, eyebrows lifted—not just in agreement, but as if to say his way made the most sense.

Carmen continued, "A problem with that is that some people can't keep up. Or won't keep up just because you said so." She checked to see if he was tracking. "What we're dreaming of doing with EVaant is definitely requiring that we go far. So we need to do it together.

"I think you're accustomed to speaking to your employees with confidence and clarity and having them appreciate your leadership authority." She took a breath. "In case you haven't noticed, the world changed. Confidence and clarity are often seen by Gen Zs and millennials as if you think you know it all and that you get to order people around. What you see as strong leadership, younger staff sometimes see as controlling—and they make up most of this company."

David spread his hands in disbelief. "That's crazy. People should know I'm doing everything I can to help them succeed." These generational differences were annoying.

Carmen pursed her lips but then continued. "They see the luxury car, the bonuses—and to them, it looks like you're in it for yourself. They believe your consumer mindset is harming the planet, and your personal gain comes at their cost."

David was taken aback. "Do you believe that?"

Carmen smiled. "Relax, David. I believe your intentions are good. I've worked with you for over three years. I *do* see how much you try to help everyone succeed." David exhaled and a measure of stress left his body. She went on, "I want to help—because even with the best intentions, your impact can still hurt us. And that affects everyone."

"What do you mean?" David was very concerned now.

"OK, I'm going to be very transparent. Please hear me out without judgment." Carmen was trying to be brave.

"You claim that you trust the employees. But you jump to conclusions about people taking sick time for no reason. You believe a bad motive when there can be a perfectly justifiable explanation.

"You suspect that people are wasting time and doing personal chores when they're working at home rather than trusting they're juggling their time but meeting their obligations by doing things when they fit in with everything else they're carrying. Or talking with their managers about changes if that isn't possible. The electronic monitoring system screams to most people that they aren't trusted.

"You put people in charge of areas, but you overrule some of their decisions.

"You promote people for their abilities, but sometimes, when you explain your approach to things, it sounds like you think they're juveniles." She stopped and looked at David with compassion. "That doesn't make you bad. And it isn't your intention to be hurtful or condescending to people. But that can be the impact."

Breathing deeply, David quietly responded, "Wow. I don't know if I can do anything about all of that. I'm not even conscious of what you're describing."

"Yep. That's human. But you're a good person. As you become more conscious, you can choose to change."

There it was again. David was expected to change. On one hand, he acknowledged that it would be good to work at that. On the other hand, he wished he did not have to. He wished everyone else would change. Did the CEO not have the privilege of setting the standards?

"And let me add a little more incentive. You know all the trouble we've been having to fill positions?" Carmen said, and David nodded, wondering where this was going. "I predict that serious work on our behaviors to demonstrate and reinforce trust will create a shift in our people. And by the way, notice I'm saying 'our behaviors'—I believe all of us on ELT have work to do to help everyone else feel trusted and valued. When that gets internalized, we can expect that new people will be attracted to work here. They'll feel a vibe. And current employees will talk it up. My sense is that we're unknowingly repelling people because of our unintended culture, but when we turn it around, we could be attracting people."

David raised his eyebrows. "Really? I'm hopeful. But I'm also unnerved by the idea that my behaviors—that I didn't even realize I had—could be having such a negative impact on people and on our business." David looked at Carmen, disappointment written across his face. She simply shrugged.

▶ COACHING HIGHLIGHT

As you consider David's struggle to understand the generational differences in his team, think about your own leadership style and how it influences team dynamics. David's frustration highlights the challenge many leaders face when adapting to diverse perspectives. Reflecting on these interactions can deepen your understanding of effective leadership.

Coaching Questions

1. How do you perceive the impact of generational differences in your workplace? Are you aware of how these differences shape communication and collaboration?
2. When was the last time you adjusted your approach based on feedback from team members? What did you learn from that experience?
3. How do you ensure that all voices are heard in meetings, especially those from different generational backgrounds?
4. What strategies do you use to build trust and rapport with team members who may have different work styles or expectations?
5. How do you define success in your leadership role, and how does that align with the values of your team?

Exercises

1. Explore the article "Why a Multigenerational Team Is a Competitive Advantage" in *Forbes*. Reflect on how the insights can apply to your leadership approach and interactions with your team.

2. Conduct a generational diversity workshop with your team to discuss different work styles and preferences. Use this opportunity to foster open communication and understanding.
3. Create a leadership development plan that incorporates feedback from your team on how they prefer to be led. Revisit this plan regularly to ensure it remains relevant and effective.

Find all our resources for this Coaching Highlight at OrgHealthTeam.com/exercises.chapter-6. ◀

CHAPTER 7

Enough of the Old Way

Immersed in a team meeting, David was feeling stress because the company was failing to reach targets he had set. Key performance indicators (KPIs) were important tools he used to focus energy and measure progress. He thought his weekly emphasis on these would make it clear to the ELT that achieving them was essential, but he was starting to wonder if they even paid any attention to them except at the meetings.

"Carmen, don't you have any more ideas for how to get our people to be more productive? We aren't keeping up. We aren't going to make it if they don't get their act together."

Carmen looked at David dumbfounded. Part of her wanted to cry in exasperation. Part of her wanted to shout. How could she respond in a way that did not just trigger more finger-pointing from her boss?

Everyone was looking at her.

She took a long, slow breath. "When I was 17, my father took me on one of my most cherished trips. We drove an entire day up to Muir Woods outside of San Francisco. The coastal redwoods are over 600 years old. Some are over a thousand years old. They're around 250 feet high.

"How have these majestic trees grown so tall and lasted so long? Not because they have deep roots. Their roots are only about 10 feet down! Imagine that—250 feet high but 10 feet under the soil. What's their secret? The roots are completely intertwined. They are literally holding each other up! Underground, it looks like one massive root system throughout Muir Woods.

"So when the wind blows or the storms come, it's like they're saying, 'We're all in this together. If you want to knock one of us down, you'll have to knock us all down.'"

She took another slow breath, noticing all eyes on her. "We could be like that. We could create a culture that connects everyone. That makes sure everyone stands tall, even when some are having trouble standing at all. We could make it normal for nobody to feel alone.

"That's a lot of the problem right now. We have people who feel like a bunch of others are watching with their arms folded, wondering what's taking them so long to do their work. They end up feeling judged—and completely alone. But we could find a way to have others link arms with them and find ways to help. To lean in rather than distancing themselves."

Some of the ELT were looking at her, processing. Some were looking into space, thinking. But David's look was different. "That all sounds good, but isn't that what you've been trying to do all along? Why hasn't it worked?" Now everyone's eyes opened much wider.

It was very quiet in the room. "I can assure you that I've been asking myself this lately," Carmen responded, doing her best to not sound defensive. "I remember you telling me something. I think we've all heard you say it a few times. 'Everything rises and falls on the leader.' You said John Maxwell taught you that.

"Well, I'm feeling the weight of it, that's for sure." She stopped breathing as she decided how to proceed. This was the moment. "Uncomfortably, I'm going to remind you that you're the ultimate leader. That the weight is ultimately on you." Everyone else's eyes were now pointed to the floor.

Carmen continued cautiously. "I'm not saying that to deflect responsibility. I'm responsible for people and culture. I just can't do it alone. I need to link my arms with you. With all of you," she said as she scanned the room. "Culture isn't just my job. Any more than finance is only yours, Bill. We're all involved in all of this with each other.

"David, you make some of us feel like heroes when our area does well. And whether you know it or not, you make some of us feel like losers when things aren't working as well as expected. And things haven't been working very well for a while. You're surrounded by leaders who, more often than not, feel like they're failing. And we carry that around with us day by day." She tried to make eye contact with anyone. "Jorge, sales are not where we all wanted them to be. But it's not all your fault. I actually thought the targets were too optimistic when they were set, but I didn't say anything because it's your area." Jorge nodded slowly. "Rebecca, the idea that we're behind in production lands largely on you, but I'm responsible to help you get the results that are needed. And Marlon, most of production is connected to you . . . I'm not pointing fingers. I'm pointing out that we're all responsible."

"OK. I'm sorry. I am not wanting to make you all feel bad. I'm wanting to make it clear that we have to do better," David said, looking at them hopefully.

"Good grief. If you think we don't know that, you really have lost hope in us." Jorge shook his head. Carmen interjected before things got ugly: "Sure, we know we have to do better. I'm hoping we can accept that everyone has tried their best. It hasn't worked. David, you have this incredible history of growing startups to IPOs, and we're all expecting it to happen here at EVaant. You've tried your best."

Carmen looked around the table. "I'm begging all of you to accept that trying our best to do it the old way doesn't work anymore. Let's try a different way—together. A way that helps each person realize the value they bring to our venture and to feel valued for that."

Five seconds of silence felt like minutes. Finally, David spoke. "Carmen . . . Actually, everyone . . . I've been losing sleep lately because I've felt like things just aren't working. Like everything I thought I knew about making a business successful is passé. So I'm agreeing that"—and he made air quotes with his fingers—"'the old way' doesn't seem to work. And I'm agreeing that we need to do this a new way." He paused in thought. "And I'm admitting I don't know how the heck to do that, so I need a lot of help."

Everyone sat transfixed. David wasn't being emotional or dramatic. He was being factual. But he was being humble in a way they hadn't seen before. Carmen broke the silence this time. "David, what you just did can give all of us hope that we can do this. Because you just showed a level of vulnerability that will be required from all of us from now on. I promise you, that was the most courageous thing I have seen a CEO do, and I'm inspired. Thank you." Heads nodded in agreement or tilted in thought. David looked around. "Hmm. I didn't feel courageous. I felt stupid. But I might understand, now that you say it, Carmen. Let's figure out this new way."

▶ *COACHING HIGHLIGHT*

David admitted that he wasn't sure how to lead and grow the business in a way that works today. Consider his moment of vulnerability and Carmen's encouraging response. Notice the power of humility in leadership. David's admission of uncertainty opened the door for a transformative conversation, highlighting the importance of creating a culture where everyone feels valued and heard. Reflecting on your own experiences can lead to personal growth and inspire similar openness in your team.

Coaching Questions

1. How comfortable are you with showing vulnerability in your leadership role? What fears or concerns do you have about being open with your team?
2. In what ways do you encourage your team to express their ideas and concerns? How do you respond when they do?
3. What steps can you take to create an environment where vulnerability is seen as a strength rather than a weakness?
4. How do you ensure that every team member feels valued and recognized for their contributions?

Exercises

1. There are some essential behaviors for leaders to demonstrate vulnerability. Learn about them in "Demonstrating Vulnerability" by our head coach, Margot Thompson. You'll find it and an assessment you can try on our website.
2. Host a facilitated team workshop focused on vulnerability and trust building. Encourage team members to share their challenges and ideas for improvement in a safe and supportive environment.
3. Develop a personal action plan for embracing vulnerability in your leadership. Include specific goals and strategies for fostering a more open and collaborative team culture. Revisit this plan regularly to track your progress and make adjustments as needed.

Find all our resources for this Coaching Highlight at OrgHealthTeam.com/exercises.chapter-7. ◀

CHAPTER 8

The Losses Add Up

The boardroom quieted quickly when Maria, the chair, called everyone to order. "Let's just talk about the personal item on all our minds before we get going today." The board had gathered for its second in-person meeting of the year, having chosen to hold remote sessions for most meetings in their cycle. "The news we all got last week that our dear friend and colleague, Murray Webster, had passed suddenly is certainly casting a shadow on all we're doing lately. I've known Murray for the two years I've been on the board. Many of you knew him longer. David, you've been connected to Murray for well over a decade. Would you like to make any remarks?"

"Sure. Thanks, Maria. It's actually almost 15 years that Murray has been on boards of companies I've been leading. He's been a mentor, an inspiration, a friend. I can't believe he's gone. The idea that he would pass less than three weeks after his diagnosis is unbelievable. I miss him," he said with a slight catch in his throat. Somber looks and nodding heads surrounded the oval table.

▲▼▲

David was driving. He was hoping to clear his mind. The top was down on his M8 convertible. He pushed the accelerator harder, speed offering the illusion of control.

Murray, I miss you, man! You've been my rock for so long. It's not the same without you. His thoughts went back to times he had spent with Murray. *You always believed in me! You never told me I had to change.*

Why did you have to go, friend?

He had turned off the main highway and taken a quiet road into the hills. Stopping on the shoulder, he got out and walked around to the passenger side, leaning against the car and gazing into the distance.

Why does everything have to be so hard?

▲▼▲

There were no other cars in the lot when he pulled into his designated space. He had stopped for a light supper and decided to return to his office. Maybe looking at some reports would get his mind out of the funk he was in.

None of the numbers were comforting. Development milestones were behind schedule. New orders were under the target. Cash burn was higher than budgeted. The topic in his thoughts had changed, but his mood was not improving.

Then Murray's wisdom occurred to him. David could almost see the calm smile on Murray's face, and he relaxed a little. *Don't sweat the numbers*, Murray had told him various times over the years. The rationale Murray explained was that new ventures do not operate like listed companies. There is no point judging the business quarter by quarter. As long as the company is building a long-term, high-growth, profitable, and sustainable business, it is on the right track.

But then David closed his eyes. Everything inside him was sensing something was wrong. Everything inside him now screamed: *The old approach is no longer sustainable. Finding the "new way" is imperative.*

CHAPTER 9

Home Is Where the Hard Is

I'm so relieved to finally see something working with him," Nancy said to David. "It's like all of the ways we've used for raising our child are exactly the things that cause problems with Daniel."

"OK, so help me understand this. The doctors are describing his condition as pathological demand avoidance, PDA.* Just telling him to put on his shoes triggers something in him and makes putting on his shoes the last thing he wants to do in the world, right?" David was trying to make sense of what Nancy had been telling him.

---

* Pathological demand avoidance is a term that was coined by Professor Elizabeth Newson in the 1980s. It's a proposed subtype of autism spectrum disorder (ASD), but it's also seen in people with ADHD. This behavior can appear in both children and adults.

"Yes. But it's even worse than that. He loves to search around in the undergrowth in the woods behind their house, finding curious insects and signs of little animals. But if you tell him to go and do it—even though it's something he'd really enjoy—he'll resist, especially if he's already had a bunch of demands placed on him that day. He can't make himself do what he'd like to do because his need to avoid demands is so . . . pathological.

"So, trying to force him to finish his breakfast, clear the table, brush his teeth, and get in the car to go to school—all actions and routines we tried to instill in Simon when he was young—are agonizing burdens to Daniel. Telling him to tidy his room, forcing him to share his toys if someone is visiting and playing with him, begging him to hang up his jacket . . . Things I've done with the best of intentions—thinking I was teaching him to be good—have felt like torture to him."

"I thought he was on the spectrum, autistic in some way. Are you saying that was wrong, and it's actually this PDA thing?"

Nancy shook her head. "No. Daniel does have a form of autism. Apparently, PDA can be related to that. His autism makes him much more inflexible about things and less aware of social cues, so his PDA is triggered far more often than it would be in most people.

"Now you can maybe appreciate why being at school is so hard for him," she choked out. "Teachers are trying to keep 25 or 30 kids being productive and getting along, so they give instructions for everyone to take their seats, get out their math workbook, turn to page 12, and do questions 10 through 15. Totally reasonable tasks. But that is"—she counted silently on her fingers—"four demands in about 30 seconds. It's like slapping Daniel on the face repeatedly. And then the teacher is frustrated that he isn't doing what she asked, so she raises her voice and makes an even harsher demand.

"David," she took a deep breath and looked at him intently. "Please don't overreact. I need you to see that you have been guilty of doing just what the teacher did."

His immediate response was to be defensive, but he caught himself and nodded. "Yep. I definitely have."

"Me too! I'm not singling you out; I'm asking you to see what I see. That we've been punishing our grandson when we thought we were teaching him to be responsible. That we've been pushing him away when we were trying to draw him closer. Like I said, it's as if everything I've been doing has had the opposite effect.

"But I'm seeing that changing my approach makes a huge difference!"

"What are you seeing?"

Nancy scrunched her hands together with a smile. "If I change my expectations, like let go of any need to be in the car in the next five minutes, and pleasantly start talking about maybe going to the store to look for some food, and ask him if he has any ideas of what we could eat for dinner, and mention that we could drive by the goat farm on the way to the store if he's interested in having a look at them, then eventually he's putting his shoes on and telling me we should get going. It feels like his own idea—and that makes it welcome.

"Or instead of telling him to get a book and have a reading time, I say, 'I wonder if sharks like to be with their family the way I like to be with you. Do you think one of your shark books talks about that?' I ask him, rather than telling him."

David whispered, "It sounds like a lot of work."

"A big part for me is to keep calm. PDA is tied to anxiety. When Daniel feels pressured, it can cause a panic attack for him. So, like I said, I relax my expectations about time. I don't nag him to make his bed when he gets up. I mention that I have mine straightened, and I talk about how nice his room looked the day before when he had it all tidied up, and maybe I ask if he's thinking he'll make his bed before we have our breakfast or after. Giving time and choices seem to really help."

"You've really done a lot of work on this, Nancy. I'm guessing you've been researching this and then testing things out with him. Congratulations," he affirmed earnestly.

"We'll all need to do a lot of work to make things better for Daniel. And we'll have to make changes," Nancy said.

"Daniel's neurodiverse. He's very sensitive to too much input. He's sensitive to loud noise. So, for example, when he's here in the kitchen and drawing at the table, it doesn't work when you come rushing in, rummaging through a drawer to find something, clunking the cupboard door shut when you get a glass down, and clinking it on the counter."

"Wow! I gotta change at work. I gotta change at home. Everybody wants me to change," David groaned.

"I'm not everybody, I'm your wife with 33 years of commitment. And this isn't for just anybody, it's for our nine-year-old grandson who's suffering. Stop acting like you're the one facing injustice here! Daniel's the one who's facing a lifetime of unfair experiences." Nancy left the room, huffing.

A stream of rationalizations flashed through David's mind, but he could not ignore the case that Nancy had made. Of course, change can be difficult. Of course, we all want to avoid it; we all want others to do the changing. But change is possible. And sometimes change is required. It is worth it. It is just the right thing to do.

CHAPTER 10
Signs of Hope

Carmen was visiting David's office frequently now. She understood that while she was primarily carrying the weight to communicate and cascade the culture mindset and practices throughout the workforce, **the CEO remained the champion of the movement**. He wanted to know what was happening and what was needed to keep the momentum building.

> **HR will carry much of the weight to communication and cascade the culture . . . but the CEO remains the champion of the movement.**

"We're seeing some amazing fruit from collaboration, David," she said with a smile. "For example, Rebecca has been underscoring to department managers that everyone is on the same team, and that hitting our deadlines is essential. If one department's deadline is missed, every department loses. So now they're moving people and budget to where they're most needed. Those silos are finally starting to come down!"

"That's so good, Carmen. Please be sure to let Rebecca know how much I appreciate this. And I'll reinforce it to her when I see her. In fact, leave it up to me, and I'll raise it at our ELT meeting Thursday morning."

CHAPTER 11

Teamwork Can Be Tough

"Are you saying you won't consider assigning someone from your team to help with production?" Rebecca asked Jorge, shocked.

"I've got my own targets to meet. I'm not going to go behind just because production can't get their work done on time." Jorge was incredulous that Rebecca was even asking.

"Jorge, you're responsible for maximizing our sales. And I have to think that most of those will come from ongoing clients. So don't you think that missing a deadline for a client that has already given us a purchase order is going to make them less willing to buy from us next time?"

He leaned forward at the table and glared at her. "I get paid to make sales. Your people are paid to deliver the product. Make sure they get it done!"

David caught the tail end of the exchange as he came through the boardroom door. "Hey, what's going on here?"

Both Rebecca and Jorge sat back in their chairs with scowls on their faces.

"Well?" David waited.

"Jorge's being impossible," Rebecca blurted, her voice tight with frustration.

Jorge pounded the table and said, loudly, "You're impossible. You expect me to take a hit while you get the credit."

Carmen entered and stood at the side of the room. Now the whole team was present.

David took a long look around the room before settling into his chair at the head of the table. "We all need to understand what's happening here. Rebecca, you go first and explain yourself."

She took a deep breath, never taking her eyes off the table right in front. "I'm trying to make sure we hit our delivery targets. I've been very thankful that others on this team have been helping. Bill actually volunteered a few people from finance to help in shipping because he could see we were paying a bunch of overtime and still under the gun." She looked sideways and gave a slight nod of approval toward Bill. Then she looked at the CTO. "Marlon, who probably can't afford to distract any of his programmers, offered some up. But Jorge basically told me to take a—"

"I told you to do your job and I'll take care of work in my area. That's how we get things done around here. We're each accountable for our own areas," Jorge snapped without letting her finish her sentence. Rebecca's face projected exasperation.

David looked at each of them, casting his eyes from one to the other a couple of times.

"I planned to start this meeting very differently. Let's put this mess on pause and pretend it didn't happen for a few minutes.

"Rebecca, I was eager to start our weekly meeting with a special thank-you for all you've been doing to reinforce our focus on collaboration. Carmen has shared some of the things she's seen and heard. Like finance staff helping in the shipping department. Like programmers staying late to give extra hours and get urgent work done in production. Naturally, Bill and Marlon have to know this is happening, and that means they're helping too.

"I remind all of you that from my perspective, I want EVaant to win. I don't really distinguish between divisions or departments. So, this collaboration is achieving a critical objective . . . It's tearing down the silos that have somehow formed in our company. Where one area only looks at itself and ignores the whole. Where one division competes with others for people and budget. Where we act like enemies within the business. And that's terrible and it has to stop!

"So, Jorge, I need you to reset and start working collaboratively with the team." David spoke authoritatively.

"This is BS. You're expecting everyone to get into a circle and have a hug fest, but what you're really asking is for me to sacrifice my bonus so she can get hers." Jorge shook his head in disbelief.

Rebecca snapped at this. "We wouldn't be so crunched in production if you'd stop making impossible promises about when things can be delivered just so you can get your numbers up."

"Hold on!" David said with a tone edging from firm toward angry. "What are you guys even talking about?"

Carmen spoke up, partly to expand the conversation beyond the terrible trio. "Jorge has a point, David, and I apologize that I haven't figured out what to do about it yet, so I haven't raised it with you. The compensation system we have is part of our problem. Like you said, we need to tear down the silos so everyone is working to make the best things happen for the whole company. But then we reward people for how much happens in their division, essentially causing us to compete with each other. If Jorge doesn't hit the targets for sales, he doesn't get the bonus. If production meets their targets, Rebecca does get her bonus."

"Yep, that's just stupid," David responded candidly. "And I'm to blame because the comp system was my brainchild in a previous company that I just tweaked for this one. Clearly, I didn't realize how counterproductive it can be.

"Meanwhile, what's this about impossible promises, Jorge?"

"Oh, she's just whining because she can't keep up," Jorge said.

"Whoa, this attacking Rebecca has to stop. We're all one team. We're working together," David insisted.

"That's not working for me," Jorge barked, pushing his chair back as he stood. "This is total BS!"

Everyone watched as he exited the boardroom and stomped down the hall.

"That is not how I saw this meeting going," David announced. "Let's all go cool down. We'll reconvene at twelve thirty."

▶ COACHING HIGHLIGHT

As you reflect on the heated exchange between Jorge and Rebecca, consider the profound impact of collaboration within your leadership team. The friction observed is a reminder that silos can derail not only productivity but also team cohesion. True leadership transcends individual targets. It is about building and sustaining a culture of cooperation where every team member feels accountable to the collective success of the company. By embracing collaboration, you can unlock the potential of your team, drive innovation, and create a more resilient organization.

Coaching Questions

1. Reflect on a time when you prioritized your department's goals over the organization's collective goals. What was the outcome, and how did it affect team dynamics?
2. How do you actively promote a culture of collaboration within your leadership team? What specific actions can you take to reinforce this culture?
3. In what ways does the current compensation system impact collaboration among departments? How might you advocate for changes that promote a more unified approach to success?
4. How do you respond to conflict among team members? What techniques do you use to facilitate constructive dialogue and collaboration?
5. When was the last time you recognized a team member for their collaborative efforts? How can you incorporate more recognition of teamwork into your leadership practice?

Exercises

1. Conduct a collaborative workshop with your leadership team focused on identifying barriers to cooperation. Develop actionable strategies to tear these barriers down and build a more collaborative atmosphere.

2. Create a personal development plan aimed at enhancing your collaborative leadership skills. Identify specific behaviors to practice, such as active listening and creating cross-departmental engagement—then set measurable goals for each.
3. Analyze a recent project that required cross-departmental collaboration. Reflect on what worked well and what could be improved. Document these insights and share them with your team to promote a continuous learning culture.
4. Engage in a role-reversal exercise with a colleague from another department. Spend a day in their role to gain insight into their challenges and perspectives. Use this experience to inform your collaborative strategies moving forward.
5. Develop a "Collaboration Charter" for your leadership team that outlines shared values, goals, and commitments to teamwork. Revisit this charter regularly to assess adherence and make adjustments as necessary.

Find all our resources for this Coaching Highlight at OrgHealthTeam.com/exercises.chapter-11. ◀

CHAPTER 12

Wisdom from Beside

David sat in the kitchen nook, leaning over his mug and smelling his coffee. As Nancy slid her slippers across the tile floor, he turned to her and said, "Mornin' hon."

"Who are you?" Nancy said, smiling. "Why are you even still here? It's Monday morning. Normally, you're driving away by seven, off to 'eat that frog' you always talk about." She was curious but savoring his presence. One of the reasons she had retired early was to just be around more so she could enjoy the moments when David was available. In the end, it became much more about being around to take time with their grandson, Daniel, but this time with David was precious to her.

"I was wondering if you could teach me something." Nancy's brows furrowed at David's words. He continued, uneasily. "When you were explaining how you've been helping Daniel, you talked about how many different ways you've been working to get through to him. And you said that changing your approach was making a big difference."

Nancy was nodding slowly. "Yeah," she said, with a slight rise at the end of the word.

"Well, first, I want you to know that I'm proud of you," he said. "I can only guess how hard that might have been. Because I've been trying to make some changes at work, and it's not going well. So, my ask is that you think about what you've done to get through the hard part and actually change. And teach me how to do that too."

Nancy took a seat and looked at her husband with admiration. "How brave of you, dear. What are you trying to change?" she asked, and then added, "But let me admit to you first that I am certainly not through the hard part. It's still very hard. Thankfully, it's become rewarding too."

"Fair enough. Hard can last a long time. I'm hearing you," David acknowledged. "I'm trying to figure out what changes I need to make so that people experience me differently than they've been experiencing me.

"Carmen's mostly to blame for all this. I didn't really even know people were having trouble with me until she told me." He paused. "Meanwhile, she seems to be telling me these things because she's trying to help, not trying to crucify me. So, she deserves credit too."

"Good for her. I hope you're letting her see that you appreciate it, because you need to know that it must be terribly hard for her to bring any of this up to her boss." Nancy waited for David to internalize what she said. "Sometimes, your expressions alone can shut people down—even when you mean well."

"Yep. That's the kind of stuff I'm talking about. Stuff I do that's so ingrained, I don't even know I do it. And Carmen keeps insisting that I need to stop defending myself because my intention was fine and realize that impact outweighs intention."

"Ouch! That girl has guts!" Nancy declared. "And wisdom!"

"She's very good," David agreed.

"So, what are some of the things you've learned you need to work on?" Nancy asked. "In addition to not skewering people with your looks." She smiled.

David thought for a moment. "She has this saying: 'Replace judgment with curiosity.' Sadly, my default is to instantly assess what's been said or what's happened and then declare what I think about it. Maybe even declare what's wrong with it. Which predictably puts people on the defensive. And what could've been a conversation becomes a debate. Or, more often, the other person gives up, and the conversation's over. Except they haven't changed their mind, they've just abdicated to me."

Nancy looked at him and eventually asked, "How do you feel about that?"

David shook his head. "Good grief! You just did it, didn't you! You held back, changed what you were going to say, and asked how I'm feeling instead."

"Yes," Nancy smiled. "Because my first thought was, 'Yes, David, you do this to me all the time.' But I quickly realized that wouldn't help you. You already know it's a problem. It won't help to make you feel worse about yourself. It won't help us have a fruitful conversation." She paused. "It won't help me help you. And I truly want to help you."

"I am incredibly blessed to have you as my wife, Nancy," he said, and he moved from his chair and knelt with his head on her lap and arms around her waist. "Thank you for your patience and understanding and love." His words were barely audible, spoken into her robe.

They stayed in that position for a prolonged moment. "Thank you," he said again, rising back to his chair.

David continued to give examples of behavioral defaults that were impacting people negatively:

- Defending or emphasizing his views when someone offered a contrary idea;
- Smiling as someone criticized him, causing them to feel he was being smug;
- Interrupting people as they were speaking, implying his thoughts were more important;
- Declaring his thoughts on most issues rather than asking people for their ideas;
- Dismissing people's ideas or questions because he had given the topic thorough consideration and made his conclusion, but that minimized the potential value of others;
- Speaking with confidence and somehow conveying superiority.

"OK, I'm sure there are more. And you probably could add to my list. But can we talk about what I can do to change? It seems I don't realize I'm repeating these behaviors until well after it happens, or when someone points it out." David was being earnest.

Nancy looked at him tenderly. "You might be surprised at my answer. The thing that's made all the difference for me regarding Daniel is love. I keep reminding myself how much I love him. How deserving he is of my love. And asking myself how I can show him my love by how I speak, how I sound, how I look—my expressions and gestures, how I listen, how I confirm I'm understanding." She thought for a moment. "I think my focus on love is actually what enables me to keep working at it. And that's a big deal. Because it's so much work—and so much slower coming than I want."

They sat with that for a few moments.

Awkwardly, David asked, "Do you think I should love people at work more?"

"Well, you might use the word 'value' or 'care.' But you know what I'm getting at. Do you think you love people at work now?" Nancy asked, with no judgment in her tone.

"I'd like to say yes, but love is a high bar. Part of me wonders if that's professional," David admitted.

"I mean this kindly," Nancy cautioned. "Don't you think that's sort of lame?

"We're not talking about romance here. We're not saying you'd be hugging people everywhere. It's not like you'd be leaving little notes with *X*'s and *O*'s on their desks. We're really just saying that you'd care enough about a person that you want what's best for them. You'd want them to be their best. You'd work at knowing them well enough that you could help them succeed. Because you care that much. I think that's love."

David remained silent, thoughts jumbled. Nancy gave him time. "You're a very wise woman, wife of mine," David said. "I need to think about this. I need to give this some time." He rose again and leaned toward her, hugging her gently. "Thank you. I'm heading to the office, but not because I want to leave you."

Nancy pushed him back softly so she could see his face. "I love you too. Have a good day. I'll see you tonight."

David stepped across the kitchen to the garage entrance, buoyed up by hope and gratitude.

▶ COACHING HIGHLIGHT

David and Nancy's chat illustrates how a leader's behavior can really shape the interpersonal dynamics of a team (or a family). Reflect on David's evolving self-awareness. He's starting to see how some of his ingrained habits and offhand comments, even if unintentional, are actually throwing up walls instead of building bridges. Examining and understanding these dynamics is key to building a high-performing and positive workplace where everyone feels empowered and valued—like they're part of something bigger. It's all about creating an atmosphere where people are encouraged to bring their best selves to the table.

Coaching Questions

1. Reflect on your daily interactions with your team. Are there moments when your words or actions might have landed in a way you didn't intend? How do you address these misunderstandings?
2. Consider a recent situation where your intent was not aligned with the impact on your team. How did you become aware? What steps did you take to bridge that gap?
3. How do you believe your behavior sets a precedent for your team's culture? In what ways do you actively model the values and standards you expect from your team?
4. Reflect on a recent conflict within your team. How did your words and actions contribute to the situation? What alternative approaches could have been more effective?

5. What long-term effects do you believe your leadership behavior has on team dynamics and individual growth? How can you assess and adjust your approach to prompt positive outcomes?

Exercises

1. Conduct a self-assessment of your communication style. Identify any habitual reactions or phrases that could be misinterpreted by your team. Make a list of the behaviors you want to stop and the impacts you have learned they are having. Use our worksheet on our website.
2. Read "Intent vs. Impact: That's Not What I Meant" by Margot Thompson at OrgHealthTeam.com/articles/intent-vs-impact. Notice any behaviors that apply to you and add to your list from the first exercise.
3. Develop a plan to replace judgment with curiosity in your interactions. Practice asking open-ended questions to better understand your team's perspectives.
4. Identify potential challenging scenarios you might encounter as a leader (e.g., facing conflict, receiving tough feedback). Write down your responses and consider alternative approaches. Reflect on how different responses could lead to varying outcomes.

Find all our resources for this Coaching Highlight at OrgHealthTeam.com/exercises.chapter-12. ◀

CHAPTER 13
Collaboration Isn't Enough

I'm as surprised as anyone that Jorge actually quit. I thought he was just mad but would come around," admitted David. Carmen listened, expressionless.

"What's even more surprising is what people are telling me about Jorge. It's crazy how nobody says a thing to me when things are happening, but now they can't stop raggin' on the guy."

Carmen was curious. "What are people telling you?"

"That he was a grandstander, always looking to get credit for anything good that happened, even if it was someone else who did it," said David. "That he would complain about me and some of the rest of you on the ELT to people in his department. That he would make sure people noticed his fancy clothes and high-priced watch and expensive car. Like he was always competing against everyone else."

"And you never saw that before?" Carmen asked.

"Never in a way that stood out. Sure, I saw his expensive tastes, but it never bothered me."

Carmen nodded. "And I bet you never felt like he was competing with you. Because he couldn't impress you. You've got your own fancy car; you dress well but not so that you show off. You only paid attention to his results, right?"

"Yep. But now I'm wondering how many times he twisted his reports so they made him look better than he really was." David was shaking his head.

"Look, I'm not saying I knew all of that, but I do think I saw more than you did. Or at least I believed there was a problem more than you did," Carmen said softly. "To be honest, I was feeling like we needed his charismatic sales strength, so I sort of turned a blind eye to the signals. I wanted to believe he was as good as he claimed to be. I wanted it for all of us."

She paused, then added, "Now that we see all of this more clearly, are you recognizing how poisonous he was to everything we're trying to do?"

David sat with his elbows on his knees, looking at the floor. "Sure," he said quietly. Carmen waited for what might be coming.

"I'm thinking about the good work you've been doing to encourage collaboration. And I'm thinking it's for nothing when someone like Jorge behaves like he did." David sat up and looked directly at her. "I got so excited about the power of collaboration that I failed to see there's more to it. Collaboration isn't enough. But I'm not quite sure what's missing."

They both sat thinking for a while. "We need to figure this out, Carmen. Let's give it some time and come back to this." He stood, and she took the cue that the meeting was over.

▲▼▲

"Gang, we're going to take a detour for our meeting today," David said, opening their Thursday team gathering. "I'm going to start by apologizing." Everyone looked at him with eyebrows raised. "A week ago, we all experienced a shock. Jorge mistreated Rebecca. And then he stomped out. Angry and loud.

"I've been thinking about that a lot this week," he continued. "I hope you have too. I've come to realize that Jorge's misbehavior was going on for a long time, and it was more evident than I was letting myself notice. I wish I'd done something sooner. I'm sorry." He made eye contact with each of the four others. Everyone sat silently.

"No big deal," Bill finally said, breaking the ice. Some nods and yeahs followed.

David smiled. "Thanks, guys. You're kind. But let's not minimize this. It *is* a big deal, and I should have seen it way sooner.

"Let me name the awkwardness," David said, raising his voice slightly. "I'm guessing all of you did see it before I did." He looked around the room. Nobody moved. "Carmen, fess up. You've already admitted this to me. Share it with the team."

Carmen cleared her throat. "Yeah. He stirred up a lot of division—pitting people against each other and creating disunity." She turned to her left. "Come on, Rebecca. You saw it too."

Rebecca nodded once. "Yep. Jorge continually made commitments that put ridiculous pressure on operations. Lots of people despised him."

"He was a pompous ass," Bill said flatly. A few people chuckled, more out of release than humor.

"Maybe," David said, "but let's not disrespect him in his absence." Some eyes around the table rolled. "If we're going to be a great team, we need to take things to a higher level.

"This is awkward for two reasons: One, it shows how blind I've been. Two, it reveals how silent the rest of you have been." Everyone looked aghast. "Hey, I'm not criticizing you. I'm saying you guys saw the problem, but something about our dynamic—our teamwork—made it so no one said anything to me. That's on me."

Marlon raised his hand like a policeman at a traffic stop. "Hold on. You're being too hard on yourself. You're right. I knew there was a problem. I should've said something. For me, part of it was that I thought you'd sort it all out. I was just waiting for the famous David Slater to save the day."

"Interesting," David responded. "What was the other part?"

Marlon let his head droop. "I was kind of afraid to say it. You picked Jorge. Who am I to contradict your decisions?" Several others signaled agreement by voice or gesture.

"See? That stings a bit," David said with a half laugh, trying to lighten the mood.

"You talked about us taking things to a higher level," Carmen inserted. "I hope all of us are seeing how you're doing that right now. First of all, you apologized. That's just weird for us. Until just recently, I don't think we saw you do that. Second, you're slowing things down to talk about our team dynamics. Geez, that is not what a Thursday team meeting ever looked like." Others were affirming with nods and smiles. She looked around the table. "What do you think, everyone? Other than feeling a bit guilty for not raising any alarms, doesn't this feel like a whole new level of teamwork right now?"

"Definitely," Rebecca confirmed. "I think so too," Marlon said. Everyone looked at Bill. "Yep. It's different, that's for sure," he acknowledged. "I'm not sure if it's higher or better, yet."

Carmen jumped on that. "*Por el amor de Dios*! Bill, come on. You know this is better. You know a typical team meeting has been 90 percent David talking. Now he's asking us. He's apologizing!" Everyone knew when Carmen started interjecting Spanish, she was at the end of her rope.

David smiled. "Well, we're definitely getting more openness in today's meeting." After a pause, he looked at Bill and said, "More openness, Bill. Bring it on."

Everyone could see Bill squirm a little. "Honestly? I kind of like it when David just calls the plays. He's the quarterback. I'm fine playing my position." He hesitated, then said, "Plus, I'm not sure I want to sign up for admitting mistakes and apologizing. I hate doing that."

Carmen let that settle on the group, then said, "Bill. You just showed us what you're feeling. That's an amazing example of taking us to a higher level." She looked at him with admiration. "You can do this. Of course it isn't easy. It isn't natural. That's true for all of us. But if we all work at it together, it'll make a huge difference."

"I'm believing that," David added. "We've been working together at collaboration in our company for a couple months. Carmen has especially been helping me—and all of us. Our conversation here today makes me realize there's more to what it looks like than I was seeing before.

"Carmen and I were talking a couple days ago, and all this mess with Jorge made us realize that collaboration isn't enough." David paused, thinking. "What else do we need to see?"

Rebecca slowly suggested, "I think it's about us. About how *we* behave. It's like there's—"

"Brilliant, Rebecca!" David declared. "That's the missing piece. Collaboration is great, but it falls apart if the leaders aren't living it. Not only does that mean the effectiveness of the ELT is compromised—and we're tasting the difference of that right here, today—but the effectiveness of the entire company's hindered. People notice the inconsistencies and lose confidence. When we don't act the way we're telling everyone else to act, they give up. At least they do when we aren't watching them.

"What do we call that?" David asked aloud, although it looked like he was talking to himself. "What label do we put on it?"

Bill spoke up. "How about leadership accountability?"

David pointed a finger at Bill. "That's it. Boom! Companies are stronger when there's collaboration *and* leadership accountability. I love it!"

David rose and signaled that the meeting was over. The transition struck everyone abruptly, but they were content that their time had been well used, and it would be good to get back to the pressing demands they each carried.

As they went their separate ways, Carmen caught up to David and spoke quietly while she walked beside him. "That was fabulous, David. Well done."

"Thanks," he said. "And thank you. You were a huge part of it. Everyone was."

Carmen smiled. "Yes, we all did it together." She touched his elbow and stopped in the hall. David turned to face her. "You asked me to help you with some behaviors that you're trying to change. I'm just going to point out that when you got all energized about the part that leaders play, you completely cut off Rebecca, who brought the idea up."

David closed his eyes and winced. "God help me," he said. He turned and walked into his office. Carmen left him alone to process.

▶ COACHING HIGHLIGHT

When David honestly reflected on Jorge quitting and why the team stayed quiet, he learned something important: Even the best leaders can let their teams crumble if they don't prioritize honesty and responsibility. Consider how Carmen courageously pushed David to face reality. Not until that moment could the team finally admit they were letting problems slide, showing that real leadership change happens when everyone consistently steps up and acts together. For top executives and boards, this chapter is a wake-up call. Teamwork without real responsibility is just for show, and creating a "speak up" culture only works if you keep nurturing it every day.

Coaching Questions

1. David admitted he overlooked Jorge's toxic behavior despite clear signals. When have you dismissed red flags about a high performer to preserve short-term results? What systemic structures enabled that oversight?
2. Carmen and the team stayed silent until an actual crisis struck. How does your board or C-suite actively seek out disagreement? What unspoken rules discourage calling out discrepancies between declared values and actions?

3. Bill resisted vulnerability, preferring a "quarterback" leader. How do you balance decisiveness with humility in your role? Where does your organization integrate authority with infallibility?
4. Rebecca's contribution was overshadowed by David's enthusiasm. How can you ensure introverted or quieter voices aren't tokenized or silenced in important discussions?
5. Accountability can be framed as "leadership homework." Rather than leaving it as a hope that people do something, how could David have volunteered some accountability for himself to the group? What metrics do you use to evaluate executive alignment with cultural values—not just operational outcomes?

Exercises

1. Map real examples over the past quarter where conflicting opinions were withheld in senior leadership meetings. Identify patterns (e.g., fear of contradicting the CEO, cultural stigma around criticism) and draft guidelines to normalize "radical candor" at the board and C-suite level.
2. Role-play a leadership crisis (e.g., unethical behavior by a top performer). Assign leaders to advocate for competing priorities (reputation, transparency, shareholder returns). Afterward, debrief whether openness or politeness prevailed.
3. Commission a third-party review of leadership communications and decision-making processes. Measure any gaps between stated values (e.g., collaboration) and observable actions, with actionable steps to close them.

4. Task each senior leader with shadowing a junior staff member for a day, documenting where leadership behaviors contradict the desired company culture. Present findings to the management team along with a plan to address them.

Find all our resources for this Coaching Highlight at OrgHealthTeam.com/exercises.chapter-13. ◀

CHAPTER 14

The Bottom Line

Bill had asked David about the meetings he had seen happening between his boss and Carmen. When he learned that they were theorizing about what it would take to make EVaant a healthy organization, he asked if he could join the next one. David was a bit surprised, thinking Bill to be much more of a concrete thinker than a philosophical muser. But he happily extended the invitation.

When they gathered, Bill jumped right in. "You guys have been chipping away at making collaboration a hallmark of our business," he said, "and that's great. I'm really impressed with the things Rebecca has been doing to get coordination between departments."

David and Carmen were pleased by Bill's positive view on this.

"And then a few weeks ago," Bill continued, "you led the whole ELT to make the important discovery that Leadership Accountability is essential to support it." He had both their rapt attention. "I'm scared you're missing the most important piece," he stated, trepidation on his face.

David tried to calm him, saying, "You've got my attention. What are you thinking?"

Bill turned his chair to face David square on and said, "Doesn't it bother you that we're kind of limping along financially?" He did his best to say it without inferring any blame or criticism. "A company can't be healthy if it's short of money!"

David bit his tongue. Everything inside him was preparing a response to Bill, giving assurance that he was well aware of the situation and that he was also very concerned, and he had some plans to handle it. Instead of speaking any of it, he asked, "How do you think finance should be included in our plan to be healthy, Bill?"

Bill was thinking, fumbling somewhat because of the question. Carmen interjected, saying "That's a great question, David. You're doing really well on engaging rather than dominating."

David shrugged. Bill looked puzzled and asked Carmen, "What does that mean?"

"One of the things that we've been talking about as we increase collaboration is how David responds to certain situations. You looked a bit surprised by his question, Bill. What did you think was going to happen?"

Bill's face went pale. He hemmed and hawed. "I guess I was expecting David to tell me I'm crazy and explain how it's all going according to his plan." He breathed loudly. "Or maybe he'd thank me glibly and give me marching orders so we could turn it around." He breathed on. "I wasn't expecting a question . . . So why is it a good question?"

Carmen smiled, "That's a good question too. I think you're right. Maybe David was close to doing something like you just described. But he stopped himself because he's noticed that his tendency to pronounce his opinion about things shuts other people down and projects a superiority." She turned to David. "Was that what happened?"

David nodded.

"Right," Carmen said. "So, David's question was good because instead of behaving like you imagined—like you've seen before many times, he asked for your thoughts." She turned her palms up, and said, "He changed his behavior to increase collaboration. And I think he's doing really well at that."

"It's so unnatural for me," David admitted. "I'm inconsistent. When I do realize the change that's needed, it's usually so far after I made the mistake, I'm not even with the person to say anything." He looked defeated.

"Give yourself a break," said Carmen. "Nobody's perfect. And nobody expects you to be. Just keep working at it. The effort alone is visible, and that will give most people reason to believe you're genuinely aiming to value them."

"Or maybe love them," David said softly, almost to himself.

Carmen's eyes enlarged. "Love them?" she asked with a grin and wide eyes. Bill sat with wide eyes too.

David squirmed a bit. "Yeah. It's something Nancy said to me." He wished he hadn't let his inner voice be heard. "She found that what really helped her change her behaviors working with our grandson was focusing on her love for him. She wonders if it might be the only thing that's powerful enough to make that kind of change possible." He was still processing her input, marveling at her wisdom and trying to make sense of it in the work context.

He looked at Bill sheepishly. "Do you think I've gone off the deep end?" he asked with some embarrassment.

Carmen inserted herself. "I'd say your wife is kind of profound," she responded. "I like what she's noticing."

David kept looking at Bill. Nothing. He wanted to wind time back a few minutes. "My earlier question to you, Bill, was how do you think we need to change our description of a healthy company so this finance piece is incorporated?"

They all knew it was a change of topic, but no one resisted. Bill spoke first. "Profit is like oxygen for a business. A healthy company has growing profit. Or at least sustained profit," he clarified. "We might feel like we're getting healthier—and that's legitimate—but I don't think we can claim we're healthy unless we're seeing overflow."

The group was processing what Bill said, agreeing, but pondering further. Carmen was first to speak. "If we had overflow, we'd be likely to invest in the kind of training that would help everyone develop more of the skills that are needed to collaborate well. I'd guess that 95 percent of our training dollars are spent on job-task skill building. But what if we helped people listen more effectively, or communicate in ways that didn't trigger defensiveness, and to brainstorm possibilities as a group, and to show value for others?"

David joined in. "What if we found out that investing in those things actually creates the overflow?"

"See . . ." Bill connected dots in his mind. "A healthy company can do more, which generates more profit, which offers more possibility." They were all nodding.

"This is very helpful," David said. "I appreciate your taking the initiative to join into this conversation, Bill. Sustainable profitability is certainly part of the picture for a healthy company."

David hopped up and went to the whiteboard, sketching an image to capture what they had been discussing, using italics for the third box to signify its more tentative status.

Collaborative Culture	Leadership Accountability	*Sustainable Profitability*

They all looked at it thoughtfully. "Let's give this more processing time," David said. "Great to be thinking this through with both of you! Thanks!"

▶ COACHING HIGHLIGHT

David decided to stop giving orders and instead ask questions. This opened up a crucial conversation about the company's finances and how teams work together. By staying calm and curious instead of being defensive, he gave Bill the space to share valuable ideas. This underscores that companies succeed long term when leaders prioritize listening over talking. The moment shows how purposeful communication can flatten rigid power structures, unite everyone around strategic priorities, and turn openness into a source of team resilience.

Coaching Questions

1. When someone challenges your decisions (like Bill did about finance), what's your gut reaction? How could asking *"What's your take?"* lead to better solutions?
2. Think about a recent big decision that was made. Did you spend more time talking or listening? What might have been missed by not hearing others out?
3. How do you tell the difference between *letting people speak* and *truly absorbing their input*? What stops you from listening deeply (pressure to act fast, pride, etc.)?

4. Does your communication style make your team feel safe sharing hard truths? How would they describe you during tense moments—open or closed off?
5. David saw teamwork connected to profits. How does your company link financial success to a healthy workplace culture? What proof do you have that they're related?

Exercises

1. For a week, track your ELT's listening habits by noting how often leaders ask for input before making decisions. Share results with the team and brainstorm ways to prioritize asking questions first.
2. Pick a recent costly misstep. Map out who was consulted before the decision. Identify whose input was missing and how earlier listening could have prevented the error. Present findings to the leadership team.
3. Create "Team Rules for Communication" or "Conflict Norms." Work with team leaders to set simple yet powerful guidelines (e.g., "no interrupting in meetings"). Test them in ELT discussions and note whether debates become more productive. Cascade the guidelines to reporting teams.

Find all our resources for this Coaching Highlight at OrgHealthTeam.com/exercises.chapter-14. ◀

CHAPTER 15
Working at It Is Winning at It

David and Nancy were at the table in their kitchen. What had started as a light conversation over dinner about what had happened for each of them that day turned into an intimate talk about David's efforts and experiences working on his behaviors. "It's still mostly frustrating for me," David admitted. "But I am noticing people are seeing me work at these changes and they seem pleased. So, that makes it feel worthwhile."

"I'm seeing you work at it, David," Nancy confirmed. "And I understand the frustration. It's still frustrating for me as I adjust with Daniel. My old patterns are deeply ingrained. I'm not sure it will ever become easy."

They gave examples of when they had managed to switch from their automatic behaviors to their desired behaviors and how gratifying it was to see the different responses. "Marlon stopped by my office yesterday," David explained, "and complained about some problems they were having with some equipment. I fought back against my natural response to try to fix the problem and just listened. And finally, Marlon said what he was planning to do about it. I simply affirmed his plan. He had this proud look on his face." David choked up before he could continue. "It reminded me of times when Simon was getting past his teens and making adult choices, and how pleased he was when I showed my approval." David took a couple more breaths. "And I realized I was seeing Marlon like my son. Like I love him . . . You know what I mean—genuinely care about him."

Nancy squeezed his hands and smiled affectionately. "See. You're doing it. You're making changes, and they count. You don't have to be perfect—*we* don't have to be perfect."

"Right," David said. "As long as we're trying, we're moving in the right direction. If we're working at it, we're winning."

CHAPTER 16
Top-Level Collaboration

Thursday team meetings had become so unpredictable with all of the topics that were being introduced, David had made some changes. First, he extended the timeline, so they had a full hour. Then he got radical.

"Thanks for gathering today. I know it feels like I'm distracting you from your real work, but we have important things to talk about." Everyone was listening carefully. "We're still having our regular weekly meeting tomorrow, as usual. That's when we'll check in with each other about how things are going, look at our KPIs, and work together to solve any tactical issues.

"Today's different. Today is more of a strategic conversation," he explained, "and we'll be having these every two to three weeks, I'm guessing." Seeing no reaction, David continued. "You've likely caught wind of some things that Carmen and I have been talking about, building on our push to all be more collaborative. I want to bring all of you up to date on this, and ask you to join in. We're the leadership team. We need everyone's horsepower on this."

David described the thinking that had come together to that point, and for the first time he suggested it was a model for how EVaant would be a healthy organization. Carmen added to the explanation, and Bill showed uncommon energy speaking about their most recent realization.

"So, we want all of us to talk about this concept. Our company will be healthy when we have a Collaborative Culture, fully supported by Leadership Accountability and sustainable profitability." David was relieved and hopeful to have the whole team up to the same point. He quickly drew the model on the whiteboard for all of them to see.

A Healthy Company

Collaborative Culture	Leadership Accountability	*Sustainable Profitability*

"You all know that I've been charged up about getting collaboration going," Rebecca said. "I'm completely convinced this is imperative. There are so many amazing people here! We have to find ways to make it easier for each of them to be their best. Of course they have weaknesses—everyone does! We can help them see how their weaknesses can be covered by other people's strengths."

Marlon agreed, saying, "Rebecca, you're doing such great work on this, and I completely agree with its importance. And, by the way, each of us being accountable for how *we* behave . . . Each of us owning this collaboration imperative . . . That's vital. One misstep will not go unnoticed."

"Thanks, guys," David affirmed. "You're all living this model well. I'm very grateful."

"But we have to get sustained profitability!" Bill asserted, fearing people might think he was a broken record.

Rebecca replied, "I'm sure we all agree with you, Bill. I'm wondering if there's a bit more involved. As I think about operations, I know we won't be profitable until we have everyone rowing in the same direction.

"I'm encouraged by how people rally together to get certain urgent things done. But I'm not convinced people know what the real plan is . . . what our strategy is," Rebecca lamented.

David was listening, thankful that the discussion was progressing well, content that his staying quiet was not inhibiting the team's generative thinking. It was a bit humbling to see how effective they were while he stayed mostly silent.

Carmen said, "That's good, Rebecca. I'm kind of kicking myself as I consider how many new people have been added to our workforce in the past six months and how little I've done to orient any of them to our strategy. I talk about the big dream, but I don't talk about this year's targets." She grimaced. "Sorry, everybody."

"No apology necessary, Carmen," Bill assured her. "We all have lots to do on this. I'm kicking myself, too, because I realize I've been making sure people in my department are clear about the tasks they're responsible for, but I don't really ever talk about the company's goals for the quarter or the year. I treat them all like fuel, something we burn up to get to the next day." He paused in thought. "We talk about the quarterly and annual goals. But we don't really paint that picture to the ground level. We just expect them to grind away." He was surprised at how guilty he suddenly felt.

"Maybe profitability is not the third piece of the model," mused Marlon. "No offense, Bill! But maybe it's only a part of that piece." There was silence.

David let it hang for a moment, then said, "That's interesting, Marlon. Do you have a sense of what it might be?"

Marlon tilted his head. "It's something about the strategy thing we're talking about now, I think. Clear strategy is definitely crucial for a healthy company."

"Last weekend I was hiking," Carmen began. Rebecca interjected, saying, "Oh, here we go. Another nature analogy!" and people chuckled.

"Yeah," Carmen smiled defensively. "I was hiking, and I stopped at a little pond. It was all stagnant water. It struck me how unhealthy it seemed. I sure wouldn't take a drink from it. There were ugly algae clumps floating on it. It smelled terrible." The others watched as Carmen's face scrunched up distastefully as she recalled the experience. "Maybe healthy has something to do with movement as opposed to stagnation?" she pondered aloud.

"Or momentum," Rebecca announced. "Wouldn't a company that has momentum be a healthy company?"

"I like Strategic Momentum," Marlon said. Bill voiced agreement, saying, "Nice! That's really good. It clarifies that the movement is very purposeful."

"That's incredible," David confirmed and went to the whiteboard again. He erased the wording in the third box and inserted "Strategic Momentum," still italicized. But he also drew a solid line around the box because he was convinced this third element, whatever the final label, was essential.

A Healthy Company

Collaborative Culture	Leadership Accountability	*Strategic Momentum*

"Let's carry that idea for a while and see how it settles. But I like the sound of it. You guys have really made this model a team effort. Thanks, everyone!"

▶ *COACHING HIGHLIGHT*

Consider the way David's team worked together to redefine their company's health model through honest discussions. They learned that clarity and alignment aren't fixed targets—they're ongoing efforts. By focusing on teamwork, leaders owning their actions, and purposeful progress, they moved from confusion to a shared goal. For top leaders, this illustrates that clear direction from the top *must* connect to how work gets done across the organization. Ask yourself whether your leadership helps close the gap between plans and results or widens it. What will you do to transition from standing still to moving forward?

Coaching Questions

1. When did you last test if everyone in your company—from top to bottom—understands the big-picture goals? What confusion did you find, and how did you fix it?
2. How do you recognize the difference between team alignment (shared understanding) and compliance (routine execution) on your team? Where does your culture currently fall?

3. Carmen's "stagnant pond" metaphor shows what happens when nothing changes. What habits or rules in your organization might be hindering Strategic Momentum?
4. David stayed quiet so his team could think. When do *you* step back to let others lead? How do you balance listening with making tough calls? When do you step back to create space for emergent ideas, and how do you balance humility with decisive direction?

Exercises

1. Ask managers anonymously: *"Can you name our top three goals?"* If answers don't match, use discrepancies to pinpoint communication breakdowns and fix how you communicate priorities.
2. Map how strategic objectives translate into departmental targets, team goals, and individual performance metrics. Show how big-picture goals turn into team tasks and individual work. Test this with the ELT to find missing links.
3. Implement "progress over profits" meetings where you swap budget talks for updates on strategic wins and blockers. Each leader shares: *"What's moving us forward? What's holding us back? How do we fix it?"* Focus on actionable solutions.

Find all our resources for this Coaching Highlight at OrgHealthTeam.com/exercises.chapter-16. ◀

CHAPTER 17
Confirming the Climb

The special meeting the ELT had held to talk about their model turned into weekly meetings because one or more of them kept getting more ideas and thoughts that warranted team processing. After a few more weeks, David decided it was time to get some fresh eyes on it, so he requested that Dennis come in to help.

Carmen felt honored and a bit intimidated to be included in the meeting with Dennis, a member of their board who was clearly so successful.

"I really like the imagery that you've come up with about climbing a mountain," Dennis said. "Organizational health doesn't just happen. It's a lot of work. It takes a lot of intention. No company's culture ever became great by accident." He was projecting appreciation to both of them.

David looked at Carmen and raised his eyebrows, signaling that she should respond. "Thanks, Dennis. I'll admit—while we're energized by the impact our efforts are having, I'm also aware of the weight of it all. I've never climbed a mountain, but I imagine there are parallels with how much hard work there is."

David chuckled and said, "I've read that as climbers get to higher altitudes, they can experience shortness of breath, dizziness, and nausea. I think I've felt all of those over the last few months." He was not entirely joking.

"Me too!" Carmen laughed. "I saw a documentary about how climbers go up and then come back down to base camp to increase their ability to tolerate the elevation, and then climb again. I've definitely felt like we make progress and then lose ground, and then try climbing again." She paused, and added, "Except I've never intended to come down. In our case, I think it's more like when climbers slip and fall!" Everyone was laughing now.

"You guys have a great attitude about the work—and pain—you've all been through," Dennis pointed out. "Here's where I think we're at. The central focus for a company to be healthy is a culture of collaboration. Rather than the typical dog-eat-dog vibe of corporate life with some people competing to be recognized and many taking refuge for safety, you're aiming to ensure everyone feels valued and part of something good that's bigger than themselves." David and Carmen were nodding.

"Both of you have been really pressing to create psychological safety where people believe they can ask questions and share ideas and express concerns without being penalized. And I've loved the examples you've given of managers sharing people and money from their areas to others so urgent needs can be met. That's about collective wins. That reinforces the idea of being part of a greater whole."

David jumped in. "Exactly right, Dennis. And we've also discovered the importance of our core values. Jorge's behaviors violated what we were really aiming at. If he hadn't quit, we would have had to exit him."

"Which brings us to our second peak," Carmen inserted. "That misalignment of values for Jorge would have been a problem if it were anyone else, but it was a cancer for us because Jorge was on our leadership team. He was a person that others looked to as an example of what's expected in our business. Except he was the opposite!" It was obvious that Carmen still had some pent-up frustration about the situation.

"Yep," David confirmed. "That showed us that Leadership Accountability is another peak. And there's lots at stake on this. Clearly, we had the wrong guy—*I* picked the wrong guy—and that was costing us more than we imagined. Being clear about our roles and about how our behaviors impact people around us is vital. I'll admit that last part is still hard for me."

Carmen added, "But you're taking personal ownership for it. That's huge for the Leadership Accountability element."

Dennis leaned toward them at the table. "The next peak is most exciting for me," he said, pointing at the third box on the diagram David had drawn on the board. "Frankly, it transformed this whole model from idealistic notions to real-world business thinking. It's all nice to have people working well together and the leaders singing the same song, but that kind of stuff seems to be standard fare in nonprofits that are getting nowhere. They have some benevolent donor or, more often, some government program that funds them because the idea of their organization is noble. And the people join because they like the cause. But they're so disorganized and inefficient that barely anything changes. They'd be dead in a heartbeat if they had a bottom line to maintain, but they don't. So, they carry on, burning through funding and looking busy."

Dennis noticed that both Carmen and David were looking at him wide-eyed. "Sorry. You might guess that I've had some deep disappointments on a few nonprofit and charity boards. They fail to focus on results or deliverables as the real purpose, content to cheer nice people to do nice things. Maybe I'm a bit too emphatic about this."

"Well, it's not that what you're saying isn't true," David said. "I'm fortunate to have had an experience with a nonprofit board that was super meaningful, so I'll just point out that your concerns aren't universal."

"Absolutely," Dennis agreed. "Like I said—too emphatic of me. Sorry."

Carmen added her take on this, saying, "Actually, I think you're likely right a lot of the time, Dennis. That's why Strategic Momentum matters so much to true organizational health. I feel like we're just now starting to grasp this on our own ELT." She paused and looked at David sheepishly. "Maybe it's me who's just now getting it.

"It's not soft and fuzzy," she said with insistence. "For an organization to be healthy, it has to be fruitful. We measure that with profit and results in a company. I love how some people say that nonprofits should stop labeling themselves by what they aren't and start declaring what they are—'for-impact' rather than 'not-for-profit.' So Strategic Momentum for them would be about the impact they're making in the world."

"There's more," David asserted. "Strategic Momentum requires clear strategy so that everyone's efforts are ensuring impact is made, but it's also about profitability. Or surplus, in the nonprofit context. Without enough money, a company limps along, people cut corners, there isn't enough margin to allow experimentation, and the old, safe path keeps being followed. A really healthy company spawns innovation. It looks ahead at what's changing and what's coming so it can adapt proactively. It has money available to train people properly and to celebrate success meaningfully."

Carmen was smiling. "Thank you, David. Your energy about this is inspiring. I completely agree with all that you're saying. A healthy organization is nimble. That requires some financial margin. Shifting to take advantage of an opportunity is ideal, but lots of people don't because it costs time and money they can't afford to risk. Strategic Momentum allows you to accrue some reserve to entertain possibilities.

"Everyone wants their company to be innovative, but that happens best when people have the time and space to ponder new ways of doing things. The old corporate model expects everyone to be efficient with their time, and that leaves no margin."

Dennis jumped in enthusiastically. "You guys are blowing my mind! The way you're describing a healthy organization is so much richer than I've heard previously, so much more appealing than I've imagined. I'm asking myself why I haven't aimed for this before. I think I was stuck in the routine of what corporate life looks like, accepting whatever condition a company is in as normal. Or maybe I was scared to dream about what it could look like.

"We can never become more than what we can picture in our minds," Dennis declared. "I'm not just seeing a mountain with progressive peaks of Collaborative Culture, Leadership Accountability, and Strategic Momentum. I'm seeing what that looks like in a company. I'm imagining how that makes people feel about their work . . . I'm loving it!"

"This is all very good, but I don't think it's the full picture. Let's take 15 minutes for a break," David suggested, "and then come back and tie this all together."

CHAPTER 18

Seeing the Final Peak

Hang on," Dennis interrupted. "You're saying that the three peaks we've described for organizational health aren't sufficient. Why is that?" The three of them had just reconvened, and David was reasserting that there was more required in the model.

"Here's the thing. If our company is really healthy, we shouldn't be struggling to find people to work here. The idea that we haven't found a new revenue officer to replace Jorge is kind of pathetic. It forces me to uncomfortably admit we aren't that healthy yet."

Carmen liked what she was hearing. "You're making a very good point, David. We know there's a war for talent—especially in the tech space—but we also know there are places where people are lining up for jobs when they're announced. Sometimes it's because the pay level is so appealing, but there's more to it than that. A healthy company ought to be attracting people."

"OK, let's parse this out a bit," Dennis said. "Use that hypothesis: A healthy company attracts people. Why would that be?"

Carmen could not stop herself. "Oh, I have so much to say about this! If our culture is collaborative, people working here feel included and valued. Imagine a sign on our building saying that. Or a billboard with photos of some of the staff, and in big letters, they're saying, 'We love working here. We're appreciated and fulfilled.' That would make some people wonder what's going on here."

"It would make some people wonder what everyone here is smoking, I think," David snorted. "But I get what you're saying. If real people in the company were saying and showing that they love working here, that would set us apart."

"Yes. And that's evidence that we have a Collaborative Culture that's working for the people." Carmen's hands and facial expressions were animated. "The magic is when they start telling other people about how great it is. That won't happen until they're convinced their leaders are living that Collaborative Culture, and it will continue. It won't be the flavor of the month.

"Even better, if we've communicated the strategic direction and the goals clearly enough, they'll know what success looks like. If we keep meeting our targets period by period, they'll become confident that the company will last. That's when they get picky about who they encourage to work here. They'll only want their friends who will fit our culture and help us continue to succeed."

Dennis reacted. "Oh my! The people become ambassadors for the business! They advocate for people to come to interviews, maybe even leave their current jobs."

"Isn't it amazing?" Carmen gushed. "And those people will leave their jobs because they're painfully aware of how unappealing those jobs are compared to what their trusted friends are telling them about our company. Talk about engaged employees! They'd be a massive recruitment force. Between the good messages those ambassadors project and the thoughtful systems we use to advertise open positions and interview candidates, we'll attract the people who fit best in the role and our company."

Dennis nodded. "Awesome. Anything else?"

"Well, there have to be meaningful rewards. People need to be paid well, but not exorbitantly. And how they get paid has to completely align with our values and our culture. Otherwise, we get people behaving like Jorge did." David said, still feeling bad that his old compensation system had contributed to the problems they had to overcome.

"Sold!" Dennis announced. "There is another peak for organizational health. What do we call it?"

They all looked at each other, their thoughts turning. Dennis answered his own question. "How about Talent Magnetism?" It landed well, and pleased looks on everyone's faces confirmed the new peak. Carmen rose and amended the diagram on the whiteboard.

A Healthy Company

Collaborative Culture	Leadership Accountability	Strategic Momentum	*Talent Magnetism*

CHAPTER 19
Culmination

Maria sat at the head of the table with David and Dennis to her right and left, respectively. As Board Chair, she had raised a concern directly to Dennis, and he had arranged for the three of them to sit down together.

"I want you to understand that I'm not angry with you. I don't think you were trying to deceive us." Maria's tone was level and calm. "Without realizing it, you were withholding crucial information from the board. We can't help you if we don't know what's really happening."

David took it in. Part of him was defensive. But he wanted to be sure not to miss what the learning could be. He was pushing back against his default to defend. *Replace judgment with curiosity*, he told himself. "Tell me more," he said sincerely.

"What you have come to explain as a lack of Collaborative Culture, I would describe as a cancer undermining the entire business." Maria sounded firm but not harsh.

"In fact," she added, "we can uncomfortably compare it to what our dear friend Murray experienced. Without knowing it, there was a sickness eating away at him. He thought he was fine. We all did. But a hidden illness was consuming him and then suddenly, he was gone."

Maria was only looking at David. It gave him the impression that she and Dennis had already talked this through. She continued, saying, "Companies are just like that. If we aren't vigilant to understand what's happening on the inside—if we don't do checks and tests regularly—we can be surprised by problems under the surface. A culture where people are second-guessing leadership, withholding information from other departments, undermining peers, and skeptical about the future is very dangerous. It almost certainly reduces effectiveness, increases costs, and repels top performers."

David nodded. "Yeah, all of that was happening here. Not on a huge scale, but undeniably present. I thought I could figure it out, though. I thought it was just a few people being unreasonable or uncooperative."

"Sure," Dennis said. "But just like Murray's colon cancer, if things get far enough along, there's no recovery. It's vital that we catch it sooner rather than later."

Maria picked up from there, adding, "That's why we need to do some screening and tests. They're not to find out if you're doing something wrong, they're for all of us in leadership—board and management—to see what's happening. To get early warning.

"We should see it like we see our annual audit. We hire outside accountants to do checks and tests to alert us all to potential problems. The auditor's recommendations are not accusations; they're highlighting areas where things often go wrong, hotspots that their experience has shown should not be ignored. Responsible boards take those very seriously. They take action to minimize the risks or rectify the problems."

"Are you suggesting something for us to do?" David wondered aloud.

Dennis smiled. "Well, we're going to suggest you take your own revelations to heart. What if you and your team were to regularly—at least once a year, I'd guess—consider how EVaant is doing on the four peaks you described. Are you seeing Collaborative Culture in the company? Is the ELT modeling Leadership Accountability? Is all of this creating Strategic Momentum? And are you seeing that the business is so healthy that Talent Magnetism is a by-product?"

Almost like a tag team, Maria continued. "Not only would that be helpful for your leadership team, I'm thinking the whole board would be grateful to see what your analysis reveals. Again, not that it will be used against you, but so it can add courageous monitoring of our organizational health."

"What do you think of all this?" Dennis asked.

David's mind was multitasking. He was trying to stay fully present to the conversation with the two of them, but part of him was formulating the questions he would want the ELT to be asking in the annual review. "I really like it. And I really like how you're framing it. It's a monitoring tool for both the ELT and the board. We'd all know it would be happening, and we'd all agree that the purpose is to look closely at what's going on beneath the surface so we can be proactive to deal with any problems that are exposed.

"It's diagnostic, not judicial."

"Exactly," Dennis confirmed. "We're on the same side. We're all aiming to make this business a huge success, first for the difference it can make in the world and also for the payoff it can offer everyone involved. Monitoring our company regularly and detecting potential problems early helps all of us."

"Thank you, both of you. I so appreciate the wisdom you bring to our company. I'll be talking with the ELT and let you know how we'll move all this forward. Then we'll update the board." They all rose and shook hands, and David walked Dennis and Maria to the elevator.

CHAPTER 20

The Gift of Loyalty

"Wow. Good for you, Carmen." David gazed at the young leader he had come to respect so deeply. She had just told him that she had been given a very attractive offer to move to a different tech firm in the region. "I bet you'll bump up in pay."

She pulled a note from his dispenser and wrote a number on it. Passing it to him, she said, "Here's what they lobbed my way."

His eyes bulged. "Oh my, that's a huge amount more than you get now. Congratulations!"

"I turned them down," she said and smiled.

"What?" David asked. Questions tumbled in his mind. "I don't think I can match that," he started, but she interrupted him.

"I'm not negotiating, David. I don't expect more money."

David took a moment. "Help me understand," he replied.

She sat with a contented look. "Why would I leave EVaant? Everything I ever dreamed would be possible in my job is happening here. And I got to have a role in making it possible. It's as good as it gets, I think.

"David, you're incredible," she smiled.

"Ohh," he chortled. "Frankly, I'm more flawed than I ever realized. And you're the reason I see it!" They both laughed. "That's not a complaint. I'm very thankful that you've helped me learn about how my old mindset and behaviors were undermining what I was trying to do. But let me be clear . . . I feel like I have a long way to go, yet."

Again, Carmen smiled. "One of the amazing traits about humans is that we tend to forgive a lot when we believe that a person's heart is in the right place. People now are seeing more clearly how that's true for you." She glanced upward to her left as she thought. "I think I've always believed your heart is in the right place."

"That's very gracious of you, Carmen. I'm forever thankful."

▶ *COACHING HIGHLIGHT*

As you reflect on David's self-awareness of his flaws and Carmen's solid belief in his growth, consider this profound truth: Leadership is not about perfection but about progress. Here's the thing: David knows he's not perfect—and Carmen doesn't expect him to be. She sees him as "incredible" not because he's fixed all his flaws, but because he's consistently *trying* to grow. He's showing up, learning, and moving forward, even if it's messy. That's what leadership really is. It's not about being flawless (spoiler: no one is), it's about keeping things moving in the right direction. Carmen sticks with David because she trusts his effort, not his perfection. The same goes for any leader. You don't need to have all the answers or nail every decision. Teams and investors stick with leaders who focus on *moving the ball forward* instead of obsessing over getting everything "just right." You know what matters more than flawless execution? Showing people you're growing. Even tiny steps forward keep hope alive. Bottom line: Nobody's flawless, but showing up *and* growing? That's what builds trust and convinces people to follow your leadership.

Coaching Questions

1. Reflect on a recent leadership decision where you prioritized progress over immediate perfection. What did you have to let slide? How did your team react?
2. How do you show your team it's okay to learn as you go, not wait for perfection? What's getting in the way of that message sticking?
3. When have you, like Carmen, chosen to stay committed to a leader despite obvious flaws? What convinced you to stick with them and invest in their progress?
4. David admits he's "got a long way to go." How do you talk transparently about your own areas for development without sounding like you're not cut out for the job?
5. When someone's trying their best but still messes up, how do you call it out *and* cut them slack?
6. Carmen illustrates the concept of forgiveness for those with good intent, but even people who are trying very hard will still mess up at times. How do you develop an organizational culture that separates intent from impact while still holding leaders accountable?

Bonus Question: If your team had to guess, would they say you care more about *looking* like you've got it all together or *actually* making progress? (Be honest!)

Exercises

1. Map three high-stakes initiatives where "perfectionism" is slowing progress. For each, identify one action to prioritize momentum (e.g., ask, "What's one thing we can launch, test, or hand off this month—even if it's rough?"). Present findings to your board with a focus on long-term ROI of agility.
2. Host a team chat where leaders share a "facepalm moment" that turned into a win (e.g., "I blew the budget, but now we're smarter about X . . ."). With a few "rules" in place (e.g., no humble-bragging, no toxic positivity—just *Here's where I tripped . . . Here's how I'm walking better . . .*), ask everyone to share their own "facepalm moment turned lesson." Use these stories to create a team culture that believes "We're all a work in progress—and that's the point." Growth stories aren't for resumes. They're for saying: "We're figuring it out, together." And that's how you turn loyalty like Carmen's into your team's superpower.
3. Partner with a rising leader (as Carmen does with David) and commit to reciprocal feedback. Every month, exchange feedback focused on "What's one tiny win you've had since we last talked?" so you're framing discussions around "progress markers" instead of performance gaps. Keep notes to document mutual growth.

4. Skim the book *Radical Candor* by Kim Scott*—the revised and updated edition. Steal the "Care Personally, Challenge Directly" hack for giving feedback that doesn't crush souls.
5. Hire a neutral third party to interview your team and tell you: "Here's where people think you're growing . . . and where you're stuck."

Find all our resources for this Coaching Highlight at OrgHealthTeam.com/exercises.chapter-20. ◀

---

* Kim Scott, *Radical Candor: Be a Kick-Ass Boss Without Losing Your Humanity* (St. Martin's Press, 2017).

CHAPTER 21

Forward with Clarity

"Well, that makes a lot of sense," one of the board members said. A chorus of agreement followed. David had just finished leading the board through a discussion about the assessment that he and the ELT had done a couple of weeks earlier and the model it was all built around.

"It's obvious that you've given all of this a lot of thought, David," Maria said. "Your explanation of what we should all be looking for is very reassuring. Let me see if I can summarize it properly," she continued, looking to him for confirmation. David gave a receptive tilt of his head and she proceeded.

"Becoming a healthy organization is like climbing a series of peaks to a mountaintop. The first peak is to instill a Collaborative Culture. That means that everyone is working together. Everyone buys into the core values of the company. And people feel safe to ask questions, to challenge each other, and to make mistakes."

David interjected. "That's amazing, Maria. I love your crisp description of Collaborative Culture." Most board members turned to the whiteboard and looked again at the diagram of the model that David had explained.

The Ascent Model

Collaborative Culture	Leadership Accountability	Strategic Momentum	Talent Magnetism

"And let's not miss that this model is more about what organizational health looks like," Dennis added. "Most of what I've read about this has explained what companies need to do to be healthy. I really like that this approach makes it more tangible, somehow."

"That's a great point," another board member said. David was nodding slowly.

"OK," Maria said, regaining everyone's attention. "The next peak to ascend is Leadership Accountability. This is a big deal because if this isn't evident to most people in the company—including the board, I will say—then everything else is moot. The ELT especially has to show everyone that they each take personal responsibility for the company's vision and mission and values and strategy. Nobody points fingers and blames anyone else. They become very aware and intentional about how their behavior impacts others."

Bill was taking it all in and realizing that some of this was only now gelling for him, even after several conversations with the ELT. He was grateful that David insisted he stay in the meeting even after the finance agenda items were completed. He was also appreciating that they all decided to meet in person again, even though they had already fulfilled their two-times-a-year commitment.

"The next peak is Strategic Momentum," Maria continued. "It requires clarity about the strategy, and this is evident when most of the employees can say what our vision is and what our goals are and how those apply to them, specifically."

David jumped in on that. "I used to think that putting our mission statement and our core values on wall signs was doing this for us. I sadly confess it was almost useless," he sighed. "In fact, worse than useless because when people saw that we weren't really following our own values, they lost all confidence that the strategy mattered."

Other board members shared how they had seen the same problems in other companies. Dennis took it further. "This is a big reason why I celebrate what David and the team are moving us to. We're going to make this company's health something we as the board can observe and discuss. We can notice, along with management, when there are trouble signs and ensure that corrective actions are taken. It will no longer be a vague or sometimes-hidden factor." Relief was apparent on several faces.

Bill could not stop himself from speaking. "I want to underscore that Strategic Momentum means there's profit and that it will continue. It will increase." He said it with such a matter-of-fact tone, it sounded severe and somewhat defensive. Dennis broke the silent awkwardness with a laugh. "Bill, we're so grateful that you're our champion to make sure that happens for us!" Smiles and chuckles filled the room.

Maria picked up again. "The final peak is Talent Magnetism. I love this one! It really signifies that the ascent is complete. Everyone working here feels valued and is highly engaged in their work and in the culture. The company becomes so clear about who it is and what it does, and the people become so pleased with their experience here, that the right kinds of people with the right kinds of skills are attracted. And the compensation system helps, but it isn't the reason new people come. We pay well, but we don't have to lure them with money. We attract them with culture."

"We're already seeing this happen." David spoke with evident pride. "Yeah," Bill agreed. "We have our lowest number of open positions in almost three years. And we're finding people who accept our jobs, show up, and jump right in. Rebecca and Carmen are thrilled with how this is going."

"That's so good, Bill," said Maria. "I think we all realize that this final peak is kind of a proving piece. There's no way that a company can become magnetic unless the other three parts of the model are shining. So that makes me, as a board member, even more comfortable in believing that EVaant is getting quite healthy."

The board talked more about the model and some of the action commitments that the ELT had made from their assessment. It was agreed that this review would be redone in about six months, just to get a close read on how things were going, but it might become an annual review before long.

CHAPTER 22

Galloping Onward

David watched as Daniel led his horse in a controlled walk past them. He had a serious look on his face, but he also looked pleased with himself. Nancy and David had traveled to Equine Escapades, an amazing place where psychotherapists helped young people with emotional and developmental needs by having them interact with horses. David was surprised that Daniel was not riding the horse, but his therapist, Lesley, told them that there are many ways for people to learn and grow through their experiences with horses. For Daniel, she explained, it was helping with self-regulation, reducing stress, and improving communication with family members.

After guiding the horse through some fence openings and around some barrels—clearly a course Daniel had followed many times—he brought her right up to them.

"What would you like, Daniel?" Lesley asked.

"You ride Prancer, Papa," he said, looking intently at his grandfather. David looked to Lesley for more understanding. She just nodded slightly.

"Do you think Prancer would be okay with me climbing up on her?" David asked, crouched down to be eye level with Daniel. After an eager nod, David added, "Are you sure you're okay with me riding Prancer? I know you're very fond of this lovely horse."

"I think Prancer likes you, Papa. She knows you will be careful with her."

David's heart melted a bit, realizing that Daniel was projecting some of his own feelings onto the horse. "Do you think I should ride slow or fast with her, Daniel?"

"Really fast, Papa. She wants to run!"

David obediently mounted the horse and gently navigated her through the paddock and out the gate. He turned back to see Daniel waving energetically, maybe just as a friendly gesture, or maybe as a signal to get going! He leaned forward and patted Prancer's neck. "Let's fly, girl," he said, digging his heels in and squeezing his knees. They sprang forward down the meadow. David smiled as the cold air whipped past the tears running down his face. How blessed he felt as he considered how much had changed in the past months.

"Thank you," he shouted, with his eyes to the heavens.

PART II
The Model

CHAPTER 23
The OrgHealth Ascent Model Described

David's story may be fictional, but his struggles are very real. Every day, leaders battle tension, disconnection, fatigue—and the quiet fear that they're the problem. The good news? Organizational health isn't a mystery. It's a discipline. Part II of this book offers a clearer look at the framework behind the story: the OrgHealth Ascent Model—a practical guide to help real-world leaders build thriving, connected, resilient companies.

The idea that an organization ought to be healthy has progressed from a novel concept to an undeniable imperative. No one wants their company to be "unhealthy," yet thousands of businesses continue to operate with painful and preventable imperfections. While one could argue that there are dozens of contributing factors, in our boutique consulting firm, OrgHealth, we've found one core cause: leadership. Leadership either allows dysfunction or drives it—often both.

For 15 years, I had the privilege of working as a consulting partner with Patrick Lencioni and the Table Group. We began working together in 2005 when organizational health was only emerging as a concept, and Pat was central to defining what it is and why it matters. The clients were hungry to discover the power of organizational health, something Pat aptly called "the Advantage."

Many other voices added to the conversation and enriched our understanding about organizational health. We've especially appreciated the practical approach that Daniel Coyle brings; his book, *The Culture Code*, and his ongoing work give us eye-opening examples of what real-world leaders are doing to shape company culture. Amy Edmondson solidified the concept of psychological safety, helping attentive leaders internalize the profound impact this has on our work experience and engagement. The incredible Brené Brown (no relation) reframed vulnerability from being evidence of weakness to a superpower in relationship building. Simon Sinek continues to inspire us with insights and examples of cultural transformation in organizations. And my friend Stephen M. R. Covey authored the definitive guide to moving beyond the torturous grip of "command & control" leadership to a generous and life-giving model: *Trust & Inspire*. Many others continue to add to the conversation, expanding our understanding with each new voice.

As practitioners, we've spent years observing, experimenting, and refining our understanding. While many focus on *how* to build organizational health, we've focused on *what* it actually looks like. Instead of debating whether leaders are working at it hard enough (and some do insist they are—despite glaring dysfunction on their teams!), we now ask a different question: How well does your company reflect the qualities of a truly healthy organization?

You've probably noticed the conversational tone. I'm imagining we're sitting down together—just the two of us—talking about organizational health and what we've learned from over 30 years of practice.

The model we've developed is largely the brainchild of Sarah Brown—my daughter—who has spent over 15 years studying workplace dynamics as part of our team. Like everything we do, it's been shaped collaboratively. What we now call the OrgHealth Ascent Model distills three decades of experience into four essential peaks.

Let's start at the pinnacle. A truly healthy organization is so effective—and so appealing—that people genuinely want to work there. Employees feel so fulfilled, they become ambassadors, enthusiastically encouraging others to join.

But this only happens when the company is crystal clear about what success looks like and consistent in pursuing it. That clarity builds momentum. That momentum creates overflow. It frees leaders to invest in people, not just production. And it proves they believe what they say: that the real strength of the business is its people.

Do people in your company love it so much they attract capable people to join them? This is the real evidence of a healthy organization.

Of course, that only works if leaders take personal responsibility for shaping the culture—and if that culture is deeply collaborative. Not a competition for budget, bonuses, or recognition. Real collaboration. The kind that multiplies impact.

Take a moment to reflect. Can you honestly say that most people in your company love it so much they radiate that joy to everyone around them? Does their experience inspire others to compete for a chance to join? That's the true test of a healthy organization. That's the elegant simplicity of the Ascent Model. To what extent does that describe your company?

Becoming healthy as an organization is like climbing a series of peaks to a mountain summit. There are four peaks to scale in order to reach the top. The first? Collaborative Culture.

CHAPTER 24

Collaborative Culture

The work world—and, arguably, the entire world—has changed. It used to be that leaders could unilaterally declare plans and demand performance. Workers would grind it out, trading time for money. But more and more, people realized they weren't just giving up time. They were surrendering their sense of worth. They followed orders—often from flawed or unqualified bosses—because that was the expectation. We once worked with a chemical company where employees followed their supervisor's order to pour a solution into a huge bulk tank, knowing full well it would mix with the contents and make the entire tankful worthless. Over a million dollars of product was lost in that moment. Why didn't they stop it? Maybe spite. Maybe fear. Maybe years of being ignored.

Whatever the reason, the result was the same: costly silence. And a year later, the plant was shut down.

After the global pandemic, when more than a hundred million people were unemployed around the world, the masses seemed to abandon the old mindset of silent compliance with unreasonable leadership. They just quit. Or they "quietly quit," staying at work but barely fulfilling their job expectations. Statistics indicate that more than half the global workforce consists of quiet quitters.*

Workers, especially those under 35, now expect respect and work-life balance. HR professionals everywhere report that new hires will walk off the job if those expectations aren't met. So leadership can only expect to retain their employees if they value the people that work for them in ways that go beyond yesterday's norms.

One key to creating space for people to work well together is for there to be a clear base of shared values. Not aspirational statements on the walls! **Values that are lived out** by the people in the organization. Even better? Turn those values into behaviors. For example, a client company committed to three guiding behaviors that would powerfully shape their culture: *Think bigger. Win-win. Fact based.* Everyone involved—board, management, and staff—works to put those behaviors into action.

It's easier to observe behaviors than to evaluate beliefs. Someone may claim honesty as a core value—yet secretly cheat on their taxes. What we do always tells the truth about what we believe.

A company's behaviors flow from its values, whether people are aware of it or not. Effective leaders make that connection intentional.

For this client, *think bigger* expresses their belief in innovation, growth, and possibility. Every meeting, every decision is an opportunity to ask: Are we pushing beyond the status quo? *Win-win*

---

* Gallup's 2023 "State of the Global Workplace" report stated that 59% of the global workforce consisted of quiet quitters. The same measure rose to 62% in their 2024 study and remained at that level in the 2025 report.

puts collaboration into action. If a decision feels one-sided, they revisit it until it works for everyone. *Fact based* is their commitment to verifiable data—not opinion or cherry-picked stats. Over time, living these behaviors has proven to everyone that this culture is worth the work.

When everyone in a company adopts and lives the guiding behaviors, alignment and momentum are possible—sometimes exponentially so. That's why the values or behaviors you choose are critical. Every hire, every promotion, must confirm that the person demonstrates them in daily practice. Your people may be beautifully diverse in countless ways, but a shared foundation of behavior holds it all together. Leaders must define—and protect—that foundation.

Living your values—and building a Collaborative Culture—requires real systems and teachable skills. You can't just tell a group to collaborate any more than you can toss toddlers into a playroom and expect order. James Clear understands this deeply. In his groundbreaking book, *Atomic Habits,** he shows how to build habits that actually stick. Drawing from his work—and what we've seen committed leaders accomplish—here are a few ways to make collaboration a daily reality.

1. Embrace the Power of Small Habits

Collaborative leaders build small, consistent habits—like sharing updates, quickly replying to messages, and celebrating others' contributions. It may seem minor, but these tiny practices activate

---

* James Clear, *Atomic Habits: An Easy & Proven Way to Build Good Habits & Break Bad Ones* (Avery, 2018).

collaboration. This is the heart of *Atomic Habits*: Small changes lead to big results. Over time, these behaviors become second nature and create a cultural foundation for great teamwork.

2. Leverage the Two-Minute Rule

Encourage team members to take collaborative actions that can be completed in two minutes or less. It makes collaboration feel easy, immediate, and doable. A few great examples include:

- Compliment a coworker—"Great job on that presentation. It was clear and engaging."
- Say thank you—"Thanks for speaking up about those concerns in our meeting."
- Share updates—"The client just approved the proposal. Let's move to the next step."
- Offer help—"Need a hand finalizing that presentation?"

These small gestures lower the barriers to collaboration and can spark greater teamwork down the road.

3. Implement Habit Stacking to Embed Collaboration

Culture-conscious leaders link collaborative behaviors to existing routines. After completing a daily task, they might send a quick update to colleagues. At the end of a stand-up meeting, they may ask each team member to share one way they saw teamwork in action that week. These practices seamlessly embed collaboration into the everyday. By weaving these practices into daily routines, leaders create a workplace where collaboration feels natural and expected.

To make these strategies more effective, another critical ingredient is needed: **psychological safety**. Amy Edmondson helpfully described this as the "shared belief that the work environment is safe for interpersonal risk taking."* In other words, people trust they won't be humiliated or punished for speaking out—to share ideas, ask questions, raise concerns, or admit mistakes.

We've seen some serious misconceptions about psychological safety. Here are a few truths every CEO needs to know.

- Psychological safety doesn't mean "be nice." It's about openness to differing views and hard questions—so tough conversations can happen when they need to.
- Psychological safety doesn't reduce accountability. In fact, safe environments promote ownership and learning. Mistakes still have consequences. Standards remain high.
- Psychological safety takes more than an open door. Leaders must actively invite input, show they value it, and respond constructively when it comes.
- Silence doesn't equal agreement. When employees are quiet, it doesn't mean they're aligned—or that there's no dissent. Often, silence signals fear: fear of being judged, ridiculed, or punished for speaking up.

Psychological safety is not a luxury—it's a necessity for any organization that wants to thrive. It means creating space where people feel safe to be themselves, take risks, and share their best

---

* Amy C. Edmondson, *The Fearless Organization: Creating Psychological Safety in the Workplace for Learning, Innovation, and Growth* (John Wiley & Sons, 2019).

ideas. When we make psychological safety a priority, we unlock the full potential of our teams—and build cultures rooted in innovation, resilience, and trust.

Psychological safety is not a luxury—it's a necessity for any organization that wants to thrive.

Some wonder why collaboration is suddenly such a big deal. The question itself reveals something: They haven't realized it's always been essential. The way we view the business world shapes how we operate in it. Some leaders believe their edge lies in a great invention—like Apple, Nike, or Google. Others credit technological superiority—think Salesforce or Nvidia. Some point to unbeatable marketing—like Procter & Gamble or Amazon. Still others believe their strength lies in cost control, supply chain, legal positioning, or real estate. And when leaders buy into that story, they shape a mindset around it—unknowingly, unintentionally.

That mindset undermines the value of every other function—and every other person—in the business.

Sure, your company might not exist without that world-changing idea you built it on. Or maybe it wouldn't thrive without the sales talent a few people refined and leveraged.

But whatever your standout strength is, it wouldn't exist without the countless contributions of dozens, hundreds, or even thousands of others. The real "magic" lies in the **collective wins** of the company. And here's why this matters now: The rest of your people are no longer willing to be diminished by leaders who fail to recognize their value.

Is this universal? Not yet! But it is pervasive, and it's not going away. Leaders who have a narrow view of who and what brings value send a clear message: The rest don't matter. Some workers may accept that—for now. They'll grit their teeth and keep the job to pay the mortgage. But more and more people are saying no to that context. They'll leave. They'll find a place where they're valued. Or they'll build one. They have options—and they won't stay where they're treated like interchangeable widgets. Their self-worth matters too much. And they're right. The world is changing for the better because of it.

People are no longer willing to accept being diminished by leaders who fail to recognize their value.

The healthiest companies take collective wins far beyond the broad mentality of valuing everyone's contribution. They crush the invisible walls that divide departments and collaborate for best outcomes. LANXESS, a global manufacturer of specialty chemicals, had a production facility that consistently ranked as the highest-cost producer in its network. Headquarters in Germany declared that unless this changed, the plant would shut down and 500 jobs would be lost. We had the privilege of working with the leadership team to reshape the culture. They leaned into collaboration. Employees moved weekly to wherever extra support was needed. Division heads coordinated that mobility and even contributed budget to fix systemic problems. Within a year, they became the lowest-cost producer in their global business. Collaboration changed the work experience—and renewed the plant's right to exist.

CHAPTER 25

Leadership Accountability

Collaborative Culture is essential. It's the first peak on the way to organizational health. But the next peak—Leadership Accountability—is where many companies stumble. Fostering collaboration is good. Celebrating it is even better. But failing to reinforce it at the leadership level? That's a disaster. People notice when a leader's behavior contradicts their words. And they notice fast.

Say we claim to value "winning together"—but then one ELT member refuses to let his team help another department during crunch time. The people on his team know they could help. Many want to. But they now see that their leader values collaboration—only when it benefits him. That kind of behavior quietly undermines collaboration across the company.

Or maybe a frustrated ELT member blames a peer's team for a problem. Everyone within earshot just learned something important: The leadership team isn't aligned. Collaboration, they realize, is just a story the leaders tell—but don't live.

Garry Ridge, now-retired longtime CEO of WD-40,* is a prime example of Leadership Accountability. He lived the company's purpose and values daily. He once told me, "You can't just frame your values and stick them on a wall. We talked and acted on these all the time!" WD-40 is a business success story—and Garry credits the formula:

Culture × Strategy = Outcome

If culture drives full engagement from every "tribe member" (as they call employees), that lifts the outcome. If it only activates 30%, it becomes a drag.

Contrast that with WeWork—a case study in mismanagement. CEO Adam Neumann preached collaboration and innovation. But his leadership was marked by selfishness and unilateral decision-making. Lavish spending and personal indulgences were visible to his inner circle—yet most supported him like a cult. Excessive partying, drug use, and alcohol defined company events.

The Formula for Success: Culture x Strategy = Outcome

Garry Ridge
Retired CEO, WD-40

Despite their efforts to distract attention from egregious acts of

* Learn more about WD-40's amazing path to success in Garry Ridge and Martha Finney's *Any Dumb-Ass Can Do It: Learning Moments from an Everyday CEO of a Multi-Billion-Dollar Company* (Matt Holt Books, 2025).

self-interest and corporate irresponsibility, people inside the business noticed the inconsistencies. The company presented itself as a worker-friendly, community-first organization, emphasizing employee welfare and culture.

But internal reports exposed the disconnect. Employee turnover was high. Many reported burnout from relentless expansion targets. Eventually, the truth emerged—and the company's 2019 IPO failed. WeWork's valuation dropped from $47 billion to under $10 billion.

Unless the leaders take **personal ownership** of the company's values and strategy, collaboration will be undermined.

That ownership includes awareness of the impact their behaviors have on people around them. I worked with a large legal firm where the managing partner asked everyone to share their thoughts openly. But when he didn't like what he heard, he raised his voice or pounded the table. Frankly, people were scared of him. So they stopped being honest. The **behavioral impact** he had completely contradicted the culture he claimed to want.

Walt Disney and his brother Roy are famously credited with bending to pick up trash whenever they walked across the grounds of their theme park in Anaheim. Walt's vision was that the park would be so clean, people would be embarrassed to throw anything on the ground. They modeled that behavior so all cast members would do the same. That approach remains standard practice at all Disney parks to this day.

ELT members interact with people across the company every day. Those people notice whether leaders live out the values they preach. I recall being impressed at a large client event. The CEO was speaking to thousands when a heckler shouted criticisms. Rather than call for removal, the CEO listened patiently, empathized, and apologized for how the company had disappointed him. Some may have seen it as a distraction. But thousands witnessed him treat someone with dignity—someone they weren't sure deserved it. It showed them that they, too, would be treated with dignity. Some were likely inspired to lead that way themselves.

You might be wondering how the more typical kind of accountability plays into organizational health. Of course, leaders' performance matters and must be monitored. But it might not look like some people expect. **Role clarity** is critical. We want to underscore that leaders lead people. Many managers get promoted because they're top performers, and they fall into the trap of thinking their new role is to do even better at performing. It isn't. Members of the ELT must stop being top performers and focus all their energy on helping the people in their departments perform even better. First-time CFOs are notorious for doing this poorly. They have a deep understanding of finance, so they earn the title of chief financial officer. But then they keep grinding out reports and entering data. Sometimes they even make the extreme error of looking at a spreadsheet over the shoulder of one of the staff and shooing them from their seat so they can sit down and "do it right" themselves! Please! All energy must be on building up people to do the work and do it well.

Another angle on the role-clarity requirement is for ELT members to realize that the default loyalty they each give to the teams they lead is misplaced. This nuance was powerfully exposed in Pat Lencioni's work, and he memorably highlights this as "team #1." If we're on the lead team, that should be our most important team. That's where our loyalty lies. We work together to do what's best for the whole company. We don't compete with our teammates; we collaborate. It's completely understandable that leaders feel responsible for the people they lead. Chances are, they hired them. They care about them. They want to make sure they get the resources they need. But if we have five people sitting around the ELT table, and all of them are positioning to get what their own team wants, it turns into a contest. This is contrary to a Collaborative Culture. And it's counter to the real role of a top leader.

What does holding leaders accountable look like? You can probably think of ways it shouldn't look! The old command & control approach conjures up pictures of a hard-nosed boss tearing a strip off a subordinate. That was terrifying 100 years ago, and it still is. Stephen M. R. Covey provides welcome guidance for doing this more effectively in *Trust & Inspire* when he outlines what he calls "stewardship agreements."* Essentially, these are collaborative, trust-based agreements that clarify responsibilities, expectations, and accountability between leaders and team members. Unlike traditional top-down directives, they focus on:

1. Desired results: Clearly defining outcomes while granting autonomy in the methods to achieve them.
2. Guidelines: Providing boundaries or principles to follow without micromanaging.
3. Resources: Ensuring access to tools, support, and authority needed to succeed.

---

* Stephen M. R. Covey, *Trust & Inspire: How Truly Great Leaders Unleash Greatness in Others* (Simon & Schuster, 2022).

4. Accountability: Establishing criteria for measuring progress and success, and setting regular check-ins, all in ways that preserve the employee's dignity and strengthen their commitment to the team.
5. Consequences: Outlining the rewards or implications tied to performance.

These agreements foster trust, empower individuals, and align efforts with organizational goals by balancing responsibility with freedom.

At the heart of these agreements is the leader's trust in the employees. The best way to make a person trustworthy is to trust them. After 20 years of involvement with Stephen, I testify to the amazing ways I've seen him exemplify this mindset and the fruitfulness it brings.

Another nugget from my years with Pat Lencioni is a counterintuitive key to teamwork. The classic maxim is "praise in public, correct in private," appropriately honoring people to the onlookers while respectfully addressing performance or behavior deficiencies one-on-one. Pat tells leaders to turn that on its head, in a way, by challenging leaders to praise their fellow team members in a very meaningful private conversation, ensuring our personal appreciation is fully conveyed. Meanwhile, he advocates that the team practice psychological safety so thoroughly that questions about performance or behavior can be raised within team meetings. That way everyone knows what's being discussed, and everyone can support that person to success. It also means no one is left wondering if misbehavior is being ignored or corporate results are being compromised.

Doing that well is not natural for most people. The book *Crucial Conversations* insightfully describes those times to be when emotions run strong, stakes are high, and opinions vary.* I've enjoyed several related conference talks by coauthor Joseph Grenny and encourage you to search for one online and watch it with the ELT. The better each of you are at these crucial conversations, the more effectively you can work together to ensure Leadership Accountability.

---

* Joseph Grenny, Kerry Patterson, Ron McMillan, Al Switzler, and Emily Gregory, *Crucial Conversations: Tools for Talking When Stakes Are High,* 3rd ed. (McGraw-Hill, 2021).

CHAPTER 26

Strategic Momentum

The first two peaks—Collaborative Culture and Leadership Accountability—take you a long way. But if you miss the next peak, you'll be stepping off a cliff.

As leaders, it's important to recognize that organizational health is flanked by two ditches. On one extreme we have fervent heroes of happiness, longing to create a work experience where everyone feels cared for and free. At the other end of the spectrum, profit maximizers analyze and organize everyone to be über-efficient. Both ends appeal to different people but are shortsighted and unsustainable.

Some see the hype about happiness, and they fear that focusing on "feelings instead of finance" will mean the pendulum swings too far in that direction, forfeiting profitability. It definitely happens! If you're in that camp of resisters, you might resonate with the term "ruinous empathy." You may find that empathy seems unnatural and like a lot of hard work. This "soft stuff" is something to be avoided, you'd like to think.

Kim Scott coined "ruinous empathy" in her book *Radical Candor.* Read it to learn how to guard against the ditch of ruinous empathy by ensuring that kindness is combined with clarity. The "soft stuff" is actually hard to do but pays off when we get it right.

Any place resembling the happiness extreme will be nonprofit—as in absent of profit! Somehow, they're fortunate to have a funding source that doesn't depend on output or impact. However, it turns out such nirvana is short-lived in reality. A responsible steward eventually requires fruitfulness, or the funding is cut off. More surprisingly, it's difficult to retain people in a job where they twiddle their thumbs. By nature, people find more fulfilment when their workdays are punctuated with productivity and meaning.

Purpose connects people to something greater than themselves, aligns teams around a common goal, and fuels the energy and commitment needed to overcome challenges.

The opposite mess—where greedy leaders extract as much profit from a business and as much value and energy from the employees as possible—has been so prevalent that labor unions and revolts have been commonplace in business history.

So, neither end works. People will abandon both scenarios because neither extreme treats them appropriately.

The answer is to add Strategic Momentum to Collaborative Culture. Enjoying the culture of your workplace and experiencing progress and impact is energizing.

Think of it this way: Would you rather be on a winning team or a losing team? The universal answer is obvious. That same clarity applies to organizational health. Everything else being equal, people feel better being part of something that is winning, something that is promising. And that better feeling makes it easier to show up with optimism, to lean in with energy, and to persevere when things get difficult. People working in a company that has Strategic Momentum can see it and feel it. Likewise, employees of a company that's scraping by can usually feel it. They start wondering about their future there. The most capable ones start looking for jobs elsewhere. People can sense if their company is healthy or not. Are employees in your business feeling energized and healthy because things are rolling along well? Or are they dragging themselves in, questioning their job security, and holding back their effort because they're not sure it's worth trying very hard?

Daniel Coyle takes the appeal of winning even further and explains the connection between purpose and engagement in his books.* Purpose connects people to something greater than themselves, aligns teams around a common goal, and fuels the energy and commitment needed to overcome challenges. When leaders take the time to craft and communicate purpose in a way that resonates with their people, they unlock the full potential of their teams. Engagement becomes not a goal to be chased but a natural outcome of the deeper connection that purpose provides. And that, ultimately, is what creates cultures that are not only high performing but also deeply fulfilling for everyone involved.

---

* Daniel Coyle, *The Culture Code: The Secrets of Highly Successful Groups* (Bantam Books, 2018); *The Culture Code Playbook: 60 Highly Effective Actions to Help Your Group Succeed* (Bantam Books, 2020).

The starting place to achieve Strategic Momentum is to create a **clear strategy** for the business and communicate it throughout the organization. We've helped hundreds of leaders craft their strategic plans. My book *The Imperfect Board Member* gives guidance on that.*

Here are some vital questions to consider regarding your strategy:

- Do your leadership team and your board of directors fully own it? Strategy is not a management prerogative. The board must feel responsible for its viability while the ELT feels responsible for its implementation.
- Has your strategy been distilled to the core concepts in simple terms that are easy for everyone to understand and easy to remember?
- Are you talking about your strategy repeatedly in every circle in your business? Every board meeting should be reinforcing the high-level plan and comparing progress to it. At least monthly, the ELT must be examining progress toward the overarching goals. Company-wide meetings—town halls, quarterly updates—should be emphasizing the vision, mission, and values. Work teams should be touching on one of those elements every couple of weeks and talking about how their team goals connect to the company's goals. It should be happening so often that most people at every level of the business are familiar with it.
- Have the vision and mission matured so leaders are convinced those statements are right for the company and they

---

* Jim Brown, *The Imperfect Board Member: Discovering the Seven Disciplines of Governance Excellence* (Jossey-Bass, 2006).

remain steady for several years? Consistency makes momentum possible. When leaders start talking about keeping strategy 'fresh,' they've already confused it with marketing. Strategy isn't about novelty—it's about clear direction.

Proof of a good strategy is that it enables the people to effectively serve their customers. I like Ken Blanchard's explanation that "profit is the applause you get for creating a motivating environment for people so they will take good care of your customers."[*] But make no mistake, if there isn't profit, your strategy isn't working. Peter Drucker put this in perfect perspective: "Profit for a company is like oxygen for a person. If you don't have enough of it, you're out of the game. But if you think your life is about breathing, you're really missing something."[†]

Strategic Momentum takes more than profit, though. It requires **sustainable profitability**. When your company can reliably generate profit year after year, that gives everyone involved a confidence to think bigger. It allows reserves to be accrued to guard against "black swan" events.[‡] It lets you invest in people, not

---

* Ken Blanchard, "How the Leadership-Profit Chain Works," Ken Blanchard Books, November 19, 2011, https://www.kenblanchardbooks.com/how-the-leadership-profit-chain-works/.

† Gerard Escaler, "Transforming Sustainability into a Competitive Advantage," *Forbes*, September 9, 2020, https://www.forbes.com/councils/forbescommunicationscouncil/2020/09/09/transforming-sustainability-into-a-competitive-advantage/.

‡ In business, "black swan" events are rare, unpredictable, and highly impactful occurrences that disrupt markets, industries, or operations. Nassim Nicholas Taleb coined the term in his book by that name. Examples include financial crashes, pandemics, political upheavals, and sudden technological breakthroughs.

just train them for tasks they must fulfill. It underwrites the extra time that collaboration can require on the way to paying off with saved time. It supports a budget for research and development and new projects.

When you have both clear strategy and sustainable profitability, you're well positioned to exercise the third distinctive part of Strategic Momentum: **proactive adaptability**. You anticipate changes that are on the horizon. You take time to forecast scenarios and plan how you could best respond to various challenges or opportunities. You recognize what your limitations are and explore the options of developing new capacities as opposed to cultivating strategic alliances with other companies that would give you access to new markets, technologies, or workforce capabilities.

The rapid rise of artificial intelligence is a clear example of the kind of disruption that calls leaders to pay attention—not with fear, but with curiosity and strategic intent. It's a moment to explore new possibilities while protecting what matters most. With proactive adaptability, you can seize the upside of innovation without compromising the integrity or focus of your core business.

Strategic Momentum is essential for organizational health.

CHAPTER 27

Talent Magnetism

We've just looked at three peaks to ascend toward the summit of organizational health. Talent Magnetism is the fourth and final peak, and it's the crowning element. When a culture of collaboration is reinforced with Leadership Accountability and paired with Strategic Momentum, employees love their work and the people they do it with. Attracting and retaining good people in your business is almost automatic. Good people are drawn to the company by the reputation that resounds. However, being intentional really multiplies the appeal.

Richard Branson famously declared, "Clients do not come first. Employees come first. If you take care of your employees, they will take care of the clients."* That's what happens in a healthy company.

---

* Marcel Schwantes, "Richard Branson Says What Separates Successful Companies from All the Rest Comes Down to 1 Leadership Principle,"

So, what do you do beyond building a Collaborative Culture, demonstrating Leadership Accountability, and creating Strategic Momentum to achieve Talent Magnetism? There are three pivotal contributors.

Meaningful rewards are a game-changing factor in healthy organizations. The talent wars underway are provoking many companies to make remarkable compensation offers. Naturally, these are appealing. But the best people are well aware of the fact that money is only one aspect of a job they'll love.

Daniel Pink digs deep into the changing landscape of compensation and rewards in his book *Drive.** He convincingly demonstrates that the old "carrot and stick" approach is ineffective. Building on his research and wisdom, consider these different ways to reward employees, alongside real-world examples of companies doing it well. And bear in mind, the best rewards are not cool ideas dreamed up by management as incentives, they're thoughtful arrangements that draw on what their employees actually value.

1. Give Employees the Gift of Autonomy

We often assume that rewards need to be tangible. But one of the most powerful ways to motivate employees is to give them more control over their work. People are wired to crave autonomy; when they have it, their engagement and productivity soar.

Inc., September 27, 2024, https://www.inc.com/marcel-schwantes/richard-branson-says-this-1-principle-leads-to-growth-success.html.

* D. H. Pink, *Drive: The Surprising Truth About What Motivates Us* (Riverhead Books, 2009).

Case in Point: Atlassian's "ShipIt" Days

Atlassian, the Australian software company, has found an innovative way to reward employees by giving them the freedom to choose what they work on. During their "ShipIt" days, employees are encouraged to set aside their regular tasks for 24 hours to tackle any project that excites them.

The only rule? They must present their results to their colleagues at the end of the day. This approach not only celebrates autonomy but also sparks creativity and collaboration. The results have been remarkable: Many of Atlassian's most successful products and features have emerged from these unstructured, employee-driven workdays.

2. Reward Mastery with Opportunities for Growth

People want to improve, to get better at something that matters. A paycheck might get someone in the door, but opportunities to stretch and grow are what keep them engaged.

Case in Point: Google's Learning and Development Programs

Google recognizes that rewarding employees isn't just about money—it's about helping them grow. The company offers robust learning and development opportunities, including courses on technical skills, leadership, and even well-being.

Employees can attend classes in person or online, and Google actively encourages them to carve out time for learning. The result?

Employees feel valued not just for what they produce but for their potential to grow.

Similarly, companies like Mastercard have introduced *reverse mentoring programs*, where senior leaders pair with younger employees to learn about emerging trends or new technologies. This gives junior team members a sense of mastery and influence, while senior leaders gain fresh insights—a win-win.

3. Create a Culture of Recognition

Recognition is a powerful, often underused motivator. People want to feel that their contributions matter and are appreciated. But it's not just about plaques or employee of the month awards—it's about creating a culture where recognition is frequent, specific, and meaningful.

Case in Point: Zappos's Peer-to-Peer Recognition

Zappos, the online shoe retailer famous for its culture, encourages employees to recognize each other through its peer-to-peer reward system. Team members can give small bonuses or shout-outs to colleagues who go above and beyond.

The company even takes recognition a step further with its "WOW Moments" program. Employees are encouraged to create memorable experiences for customers, and those efforts are celebrated company-wide. This kind of recognition doesn't just reward employees—it reinforces the company's mission and values.

4. Link Rewards to Purpose

Purpose is one of the most powerful motivators, yet it's often overlooked in traditional reward systems. Employees need to see how their work connects to something bigger than themselves. This reinforces what we covered earlier when we showed how Strategic Momentum is fueled by engagement linked to purpose. Incorporating it into the reward system is even better!

Case in Point: Patagonia's Mission-Driven Perks

Patagonia, the outdoor clothing company, excels at linking rewards to its purpose. Employees are encouraged to take part in the company's environmental mission through programs like "Environmental Internship," which allows them to work for an environmental nonprofit for up to two months while still receiving full pay.

By aligning rewards with its values, Patagonia motivates employees to not only perform well but also stay deeply connected to the company's mission.

Similarly, Melanie Perkins, the cofounder/CEO of Canva, focuses on purpose-driven leadership, ensuring the company's culture aligns with the values of its employees, particularly younger generations. She promotes social impact initiatives and inclusivity as part of the company's ethos.

5. Offer Flexibility as a Reward

Time is the ultimate currency, and more organizations are recognizing this by offering flexibility as a reward. Employees value the freedom to balance work with their personal lives, and flexibility shows trust and respect.

Case in Point: HubSpot's "Unplugged" Days

HubSpot, a leader in inbound marketing, has embraced flexibility as a key reward. The company offers "HubSpot Unplugged" days—dedicated time off to help employees recharge without guilt or interruptions.

Additionally, HubSpot's remote work policy gives employees the freedom to work from anywhere. The company believes that rewarding people with trust and flexibility leads to higher satisfaction and better results—a philosophy that's clearly working, given its high employee retention rates.

6. Personalize Rewards

Not all employees are motivated by the same things. Some value public recognition, while others might prefer a quiet "thank you." Personalized rewards show employees that you understand and respect their unique preferences.

Case in Point: Deloitte's "Green Dot Rewards"

Deloitte's "Green Dot Rewards" program allows employees to choose their rewards from a variety of options, such as gift cards, extra time off, or donations to charity.

This flexibility ensures that rewards feel meaningful to the individual, increasing their motivational impact. It's a reminder that "one size fits all" doesn't work when it comes to recognizing employees.

7. Reward the Journey, Not Just the Outcome

Traditional rewards often focus on outcomes—hitting sales targets, completing projects, or winning clients. But organizations that reward effort and learning, even when the results fall short, create a culture where employees feel safe to take risks and innovate.

Case in Point: WD-40's "Learning Moments"

At WD-40, the company reframes mistakes as "learning moments." Instead of punishing failure, they celebrate the effort and the lessons learned. This approach motivates employees to experiment and push boundaries without fear of retribution.

I've elaborated at length about meaningful rewards because most companies have such limited and counterproductive compensation systems. As David realized in our story, what many leaders presume will incentivize people to do their best actually creates competitive and negative environments that cause the opposite outcome. Be brave! Critique what you're doing about compensation and find ways to raise this to a whole new level.

As we showed a moment ago, meaningful rewards can powerfully drive the next contributor to Talent Magnetism because they motivate **high engagement**. This applies in some degree to all peaks of the Ascent Model, but this is the peak when it must become a principal objective. Intuit is renowned for leading the way in employee engagement, and it's evident in the fact that up to 93% of staff consider it a great place to work compared to the national average of 57%. Employees highlight the company's focus on their well-being, work-life balance, and career growth as reasons for their job satisfaction. When people feel valued and that the work they're doing matters, they engage more fully. Microsoft has rebounded in their effectiveness with high engagement, and Apple and Cisco get top marks in this area.

The third contributor to Talent Magnetism is **best-fit attraction**. This means that the company has figured out how to attract people who truly fit their culture and the role that's offered.

Many companies are trying so hard to attract more candidates, they're making it more difficult for the right people to know if they'd fit. When core values are developed with a PR mindset, it will mean people who accept jobs end up surprised when the work setting is unlike what was communicated. Essentially, it's false advertising. It's counterproductive.

Healthy companies focus their time and resources on *being* healthy, not on projecting that image. When the people who already work at your business enjoy it, they make it better and they tell people how great it is. They become authentic ambassadors. Most of this is a by-product of mastering the first three peaks of the Ascent Model. But developing ways to systematically select and retain the right people with the right attitudes for your company and the right skills for their role greatly increases everyone's fulfillment. The new person rejoices to be doing what makes them most alive. The people all around them find it easier to help them climb the learning curve because they seem to really fit. The new person seems to "get us," they all think, because there's a values alignment. The new person seems to "know what they're doing," everyone thinks, because the screening system ensured that would be the case.

Of all the companies we've seen, Southwest Airlines stands out for how thoughtfully they screen people when hiring. They've created interview exercises that put candidates to be flight attendants in situations that expose their natural responses and their core beliefs. For example, imagine being in a group that's asked to meet at 10 AM sharp in a certain room, only to find the door locked and no one around who knows what's supposed to happen. And picture how you'd react when someone shows up and unlocks the door . . . wearing pajamas! Then you're instructed to take a seat and put anything you have under the seat in front of you.

This is a very important part of the interview system. All of this is being watched secretly. Because they want to know they will be hiring people who already find fun and act hospitably, even under pressure. They want people who show a sense of urgency but also put other people first. It's important that anyone hired as a flight attendant pays attention to detail and safety. All these behaviors are tied to Southwest's core values. If you ask people in an interview if they believe in those values, of course people will say yes. They want the job. But Southwest knows they can't reliably train people to change their default behaviors or beliefs. Their hiring system must discover if the candidates have the desired behaviors already. Considering that average flight attendant tenure in the US is between one and two years, Southwest knows that picking the right people from the start is well worth the effort.

As a leader, find ways to detect what your job candidates already believe about the values and guiding behaviors your company has prioritized. Everything will be easier as you support the people you hire to success because their fundamental behaviors will be automatically aligned with your culture. The work experience they have as a result will be far more positive. And that will become evident to the point that it attracts talent to your company.

CHAPTER 28

The Ascent Is Complete

We've talked about the four peaks to climb so a company can be healthy. To summarize, the peaks and the focus areas for each are:

Collaborative Culture

- Lived values
- Psychological safety
- Collective wins

Leadership Accountability

- Personal ownership
- Behavioral impact
- Role clarity

Strategic Momentum

- Clear strategy
- Sustainable profitability
- Proactive adaptability

Talent Magnetism

- Meaningful rewards
- High engagement
- Best-fit attraction

The graphic below illustrates the Ascent Model and shows how the peaks fit together.

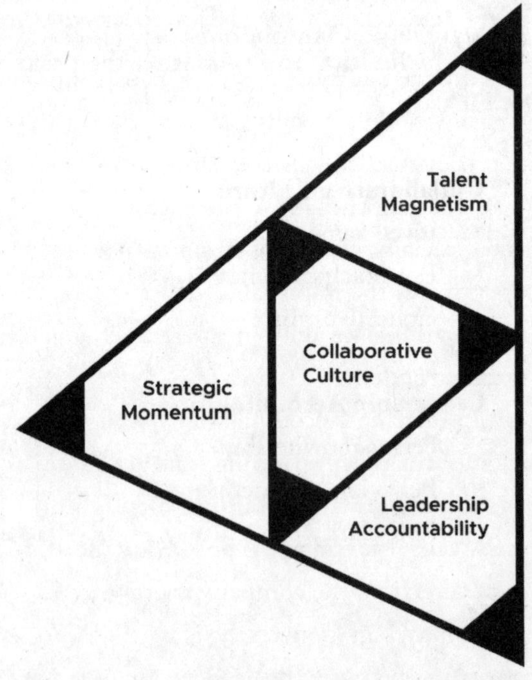

The OrgHealth Ascent Model

We call Collaborative Culture the essential ***core***. Everything depends on this. It's central to every aspect of organizational health, so it's in the center of our model.

You'll notice that each peak is a triangle, pointing somewhere and collectively pointing up and to the right. In contrast to all the other triangles with a tall point on the top, Collaborative Culture has that point on the bottom, going downward. The reason is that it's backward for most leaders to slow down, invest relationally, respond to what's important before it becomes urgent, and nurture the ground so "culture" can grow. This is the one place where an "onward and upward" mentality will not serve. Only one out of the four areas (peaks) requires that approach, but most people would prefer it be zero (because the business world generally rewards onward and upward only).

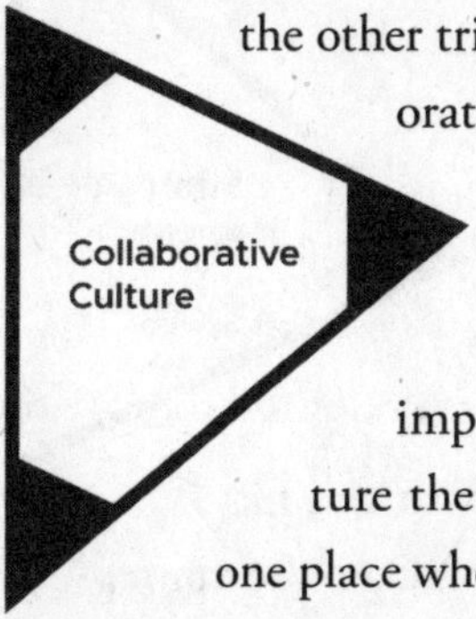

Collaborative
Culture

There are tabs in the corners of the triangles, differentiating each and emphasizing a key aspect. Collaborative Culture stands out especially, with tabs in all corners rather than just one. This underscores the importance of applying a collaborative mindset to everything we do—in every direction in the organizational structure.

Leadership Accountability is the ***pivot*** point. It's the crux that everything rests on and turns on, and the tab at the bottom highlights this. When the triangle is pointed in the right direction, the company is growing and improving. Conversely, if its trajectory is negative—because the leaders are not operating in alignment with their strategy and values and with each

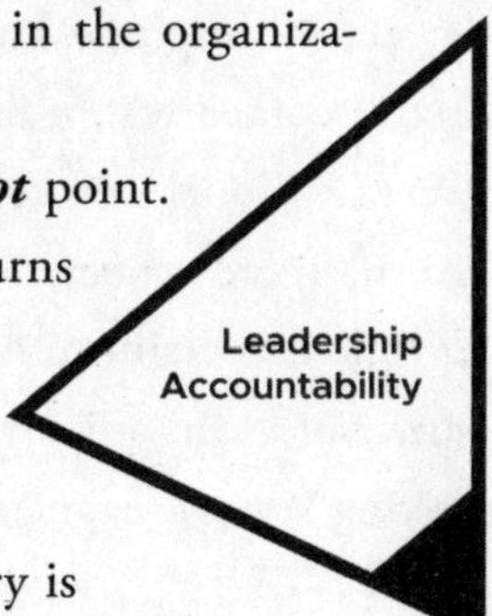

Leadership
Accountability

other—the entire business goes downward. It's also at the bottom of the entire graphic because how the leaders behave is the foundation of health and culture for a company. People involved in small or early-stage businesses will observe that their culture is essentially a reflection of the CEO/founder's culture. Too often, the leader doesn't realize this, and they let their default behaviors—good and bad—shape the company. With intentional accountability, this can be a very positive force.

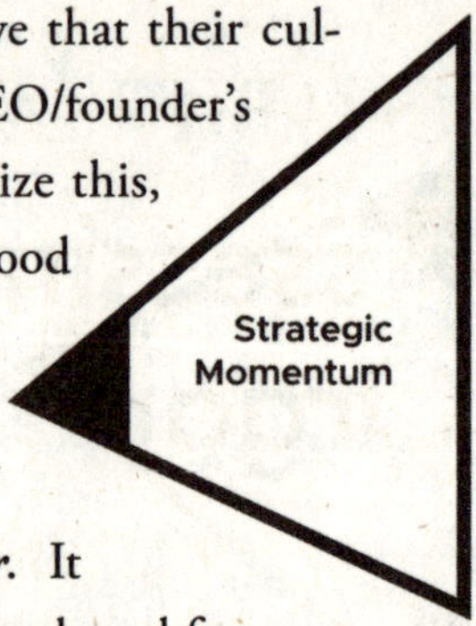

Strategic Momentum

Strategic Momentum is the ***rudder***. It sets the course, both for the company's growth and for the potential health of the business. In the image, the tab represents that rudder, steering the ship forward (moving to the right). Without strategic clarity, people working in the company flounder; without momentum, people lose heart.

The section at the top is Talent Magnetism. It's a ***beacon***, lifted up and lit by the other three elements. The tab in the top corner symbolizes that light. It's impossible to achieve without the sustained forces that each peak enables. To a large degree, the brightness of this light is the measure of the company's health. In this way, the Ascent Model makes organizational health more concrete and objective. Anyone can claim to have a healthy company, but it can quickly be confirmed or refuted by looking at how magnetic it is for talent.

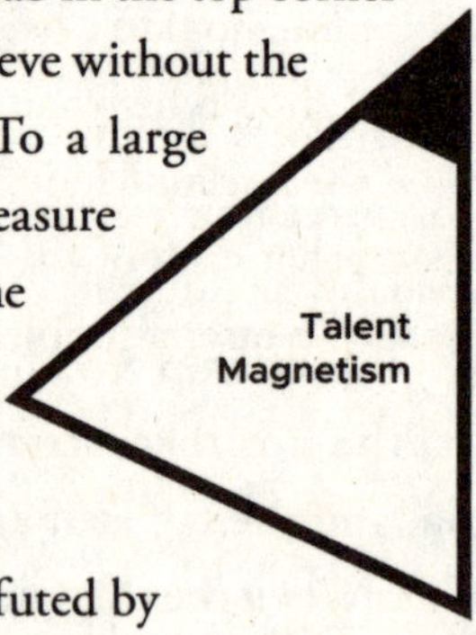

Talent Magnetism

CHAPTER 29

Assessing Your Organization's Health

People are implicitly judging whether their company is healthy or not. We want it to be easy for everyone to recognize the answer to that query and do so in a way that leaves little to debate. The question shouldn't be whether you have organizational health or not, it should be what you can do to make it better.

The Ascent Model is actually quite relatable. People can appreciate what each of the peaks looks like. But to make it more concrete, we offer a simple tool to help you know what to look for.

Ascent Scorecard

Take 15 minutes and do a quick assessment of your own company. Simply check off the descriptors that follow that are true in your business. Be hard on yourself. (Everyone working there will be!) Add up the scores as shown.

Visit OrgHealthTeam.com/ascent.scorecard to use our online assessment that automatically calculates your scores.

Collaborative Culture

- ○ Most people working in the business look for ways to help their colleagues.
- ○ The CEO fosters a safe space in leadership meetings for diverse opinions, tough questions, and admitting mistakes.
- ○ The company's core values are exemplified by each of the members of the ELT, especially by the CEO.
- ○ Individual, team, and company goals are aligned to promote unity and collaboration.
- ○ Teams from various departments work together on projects, with occasional reassignments to maximize impact.
- ○ Everyone working in the business sees how their contribution counts and feels appreciated.
- ○ The work environments, both physical and digital, are designed to facilitate interaction and teamwork throughout the company.
- ○ The process for hiring includes proven ways to confirm that candidates already live the core values of the company rather than hoping they'll learn to do so.
- ○ Employees receive training to improve skills like communication, feedback, and conflict resolution.
- ○ The ELT prioritizes company-wide objectives over departmental ones.

____ Score for *Collaborative Culture*

Leadership Accountability

- The CEO consistently "walks the talk" by living out the core values and reinforcing the strategic priorities.
- Senior leaders speak to and about each other with respect.
- Each person on the ELT is very clear about their role and understands their prime responsibility is to lead, not to perform tasks.
- The senior leaders admit mistakes, apologize, and take corrective action to prevent future issues.
- ELT members effectively communicate by modeling desired behaviors.
- The ELT delegates appropriately, empowering team members with clear authority and responsibility without micromanaging.
- Leaders take responsibility and avoid blaming others.
- People in the company follow the leaders because of their influence and example—not because of the power in their positions.
- ELT members constantly invite input and feedback from peers and employees.
- Clear reporting systems keep the ELT informed about strategic progress, enabling prompt action on concerns or delays.

____ Score for *Leadership Accountability*

Strategic Momentum

- There is a clear strategy for the business.
- The business reliably generates profits.
- The ELT is fully aligned and committed to the company's strategy.
- The company is known for delivering value promptly.
- The company forms alliances to access new markets, technologies, and skills, enhancing growth and strategic positioning.
- Ongoing efforts to refine work practices and processes boost productivity.
- Potential risks are anticipated, with plans ready to address issues swiftly.
- The company prioritizes customer needs and feedback to keep offerings relevant and competitive.
- Employees receive timely information about progress on strategic priorities, enabling informed decisions.
- The company maintains financial reserves, providing flexibility for future opportunities.

____ Score for *Strategic Momentum*

Talent Magnetism

- ○ The company consistently attracts qualified candidates, even when other businesses struggle to fill positions.
- ○ Employees generally have a positive attitude and are easy to work with.
- ○ The company ensures fair and up-to-date pay for all employees.
- ○ The necessary skills for each position are well defined, facilitating effective hiring.
- ○ The company attracts suitable candidates without needing to increase pay levels.
- ○ The culture in the company makes employees believe it's a great place to work.
- ○ Team members are willing to go above and beyond in their roles.
- ○ The company has thoughtfully created a mix of ways to reward employees for their good work.
- ○ The company makes it easy and worthwhile for employees to refer qualified candidates from their networks.
- ○ Good people stay at the company for a long time, minimizing turnover issues.

____ Score for *Talent Magnetism*

____ Total Score for All Four Peaks

Interpreting Your Scores

For each of the Ascent Model peaks:

- If the score is 7 or higher, you can celebrate that this aspect of your company's health is strong. Now you know where you can focus energy to make it even better.
- If the score is 4 to 6, build on the start that's already evident. Pick a couple of ways you will improve that peak in the year ahead.
- If the score is 3 or lower, accept your reality! It is critical that you invest in your company's health immediately.

For your total of all four peaks:

- A score of 30+ is great! Keep up the good work and challenge yourselves to make strategic improvements.
- A score of 21 to 29 is commendable. Whether one peak is comparatively low and needs focused attention or each are fair and could benefit from special effort, it will be worthwhile.
- A score of 20 or lower signals serious attention must be given to your organizational health. The best way to make marked improvement will be to engage an external firm to guide your efforts.

CHAPTER 30

The Truth About Imperfection

Perhaps you've read this book, and a couple of imperfect CEOs have come to mind. Maybe even the one you're working for now! Or perhaps you're a CEO, and you've noticed more of your own imperfections.

Good for you! Here's the simple truth: We're all imperfect. The real question is: Will we ignore our imperfections and resist change, or will we face them honestly and work to improve? Will we simply complain about the flaws of leaders around us, or will we become agents of learning and change? Will we recognize that our natural default behaviors are powerful—and that forming new patterns usually requires help and support from others?

We hope you're blessed with colleagues like the ones David had in our story. Carmen's leadership style was very different from David's—and that was good for him and good for EVaant. How fortunate he was that Carmen pushed past the power dynamics and gender biases that so often stifle voices closest to leadership. It's remarkable that Bill, despite his long-standing loyalty to David, didn't hesitate to challenge him when needed and supported the changes the company required. The way the team worked together—even through difficulty and disappointment—to become the best versions of themselves is inspiring. And how incredible that David's board showed patience with his imperfections and supported his growth as the demands on him evolved.

Together, they were working to reshape the culture to fit the real world we live in—a world that looks very different from the more familiar and predictable one David experienced earlier in his leadership journey. Candidly, it's very different from my earlier leadership experiences too. Maybe the same is true for you. Or maybe you're newer to leadership, and you've been frustrated by how slow others have been to recognize the need for change. Our hope is that this book, and the Ascent Model, can help all of us move forward to make the changes needed so that everyone in our organizations can experience purposeful, rewarding work in healthy environments. Be the leader who makes the climb. Start with yourself. Start today.

SOURCES AND INSPIRATIONS

The following books, articles, and podcasts were valuable sources for the material shared in this book.

Blanchard, Ken. *Leading at a Higher Level: Blanchard on Leadership and Creating High Performing Organizations.* 3rd ed. FT Press, 2018.

Branson, Richard. *The Virgin Way: Everything I Know About Leadership.* Portfolio, 2014.

Brown, Brené. *Daring Greatly: How the Courage to Be Vulnerable Transforms the Way We Live, Love, Parent, and Lead.* Gotham Books, 2012.

Brown, Jim. *The Imperfect Board Member: Discovering the Seven Disciplines of Governance Excellence.* Jossey-Bass, 2006. (New edition forthcoming, 2026).

Clear, James. *Atomic Habits: An Easy & Proven Way to Build Good Habits & Break Bad Ones.* Avery, 2018.

Covey, Stephen M. R. *The Speed of Trust: The One Thing That Changes Everything.* Free Press, 2006.

Covey, Stephen M. R. *Trust & Inspire: How Truly Great Leaders Unleash Greatness in Others.* Simon & Schuster, 2022.

Coyle, Daniel. *The Culture Code Playbook: 60 Highly Effective Actions to Help Your Group Succeed.* Bantam Books, 2020.

Coyle, Daniel. *The Culture Code: The Secrets of Highly Successful Groups.* Bantam Books, 2018.

Drucker, Peter F. *Management: Tasks, Responsibilities, Practices.* Harper & Row, 1973.

Edmondson, Amy C. *The Fearless Organization: Creating Psychological Safety in the Workplace for Learning, Innovation, and Growth.* John Wiley & Sons, 2019.

Freiberg, Kevin, and Jackie Freiberg. *Nuts!: Southwest Airlines' Crazy Recipe for Business and Personal Success.* Bard Press, 1996.

Gallup. *State of the Global Workplace: 2025 Report.* Gallup, 2025. https://www.gallup.com/workplace/349484/state-of-the-global-workplace.aspx.

Grant, Adam. "The 4 Deadly Sins of Work Culture." *WorkLife* (podcast), June 21, 2022. https://link.chtbl.com/pa8OMU25.

Grenny, Joseph, Kerry Patterson, Ron McMillan, Al Switzler, and Emily Gregory. *Crucial Conversations: Tools for Talking When Stakes Are High.* 3rd ed. McGraw-Hill, 2021.

Leblanc, Jeff. "Gen Z Isn't Quiet Quitting. They're Rejecting Outdated Leadership." *Fast Company*, February 24, 2025. https://www.fastcompany.com/91281732/gen-z-isnt-quiet-quitting-theyre-rejecting-outdated-leadership.

Lencioni, Patrick. *The Advantage: Why Organizational Health Trumps Everything Else in Business.* Jossey-Bass, 2012.

Lencioni, Patrick. *The Five Dysfunctions of a Team: A Leadership Fable.* Jossey-Bass, 2002.

Lin, Luona, Juliana Horowitz, and Richard Fry. "Most Americans Feel Good About Their Job Security but Not Their Pay." Pew Research Center, December 10, 2024. https://www.pewresearch.org/social-trends/2024/12/10/most-americans-feel-good-about-their-job-security-but-not-their-pay/

Magee, Shekinah "Ki." "Why a Multigenerational Team Is a Competitive Advantage." *Forbes*, January 16, 2025. https://www.forbes.com/councils/forbescoachescouncil/2025/01/16/why-a-multigenerational-team-is-a-competitive-advantage/.

Pink, Daniel H. *Drive: The Surprising Truth About What Motivates Us.* Riverhead Books, 2009.

Ravid, Daniel M., Jerod C. White, David L. Tomczak, Ahleah F. Miles, and Tara S. Behrend. "A Meta-Analysis of the Effects of Electronic Performance Monitoring on Work Outcomes." *Personnel Psychology* 75, no. 2 (2022): 251–288. https://doi.org/10.1111/peps.12514.

Ridge, Garry, and Martha Finney. *Any Dumb-Ass Can Do It: Learning Moments from an Everyday CEO of a Multi-Billion-Dollar Company.* Matt Holt Books, 2025.

Scott, Kim. *Radical Candor: Be a Kick-Ass Boss Without Losing Your Humanity.* St. Martin's Press, 2017.

Sinek, Simon. *Leaders Eat Last: Why Some Teams Pull Together and Others Don't.* Portfolio, 2014.

Taleb, Nassim Nicholas. *The Black Swan: The Impact of the Highly Improbable.* Random House, 2007.

Thompson, Margot. "Demonstrating Vulnerability." OrgHealth Team, January 21, 2026. https://www.orghealthteam.com/articles/demonstrating-vulnerability.

Thompson, Margot. "Intent vs. Impact: That's Not What I Meant." OrgHealth Team Articles, February 18, 2026. https://www.orghealthteam.com/articles/thats-not-what-i-meant.

Tracy, Brian. *Eat That Frog! 21 Great Ways to Stop Procrastinating and Get More Done in Less Time.* Berrett-Koehler Publishers, 2001.

Worklytics. "How Employee Tracking Hurts Morale and Productivity." *Worklytics*, March 7, 2025. https://www.worklytics.co/blog/how-employee-tracking-hurts-morale-and-productivity.

ACKNOWLEDGMENTS

This book is the fruit of incredible collaboration. While the book idea and the story are mine, the final product is so much more than one person could create. I'm forever grateful for the contributions and encouragement that have made it possible.

First, to the amazing people on our team, thank you for your ideas, input, improvements, and patience. As described in Part II, the underlying model is primarily conceived by Sarah Brown. Margot Thompson, a master coach of executives, skillfully contributed the Coaching Highlights that bring practical depth to the book. Everyone on the team read and reread drafts, helping refine both the story and the commentary on organizational health.

I'm blessed to have generous friends and clients who read one—or in some cases, multiple—versions of the book and offered valuable suggestions, sharp corrections, and priceless encouragement. I pour out heartfelt thanks to Jenny Hurlburt, Alain Vachon, Katie Brown, Larry Wood, Edna Lopez, Mary Lynn McPherson, Len Kahn, Barry Slauenwhite, Bill Koornstra, Peter Mullen, Freda Molenkamp-Oudman, Adam Durso, Rosa Romero, Sarah Stanley, David Hopper, Brandon Richardson, Shree Sharma, and Jonathan and Meaghan Brown.

Special thanks go to a few authors whose work and wisdom have made a profound impact on business leadership—and who graciously offered their input on this project. Dave Ramos was among the first to pour accelerant on early sparks. Garry Ridge shared invaluable experience, both as an author and as a business leader. Stephen M. R. Covey brought fresh perspective and encouragement at crucial points. I treasure our friendship.

Matt Holt and his remarkable team at BenBella Books made this project a joy to pursue. I'm grateful to be part of the Matt Holt Books family!

To Karen, my wife and life partner—thank you for the patience and encouragement you showed through late nights, early mornings, and endless drafts. You helped me remember that the most important leadership happens closest to home.

I also declare my deep gratitude to God. In a very real way, I experienced His still, small voice—prompting, envisioning, and propelling both the writing and the momentum of this undertaking.

Finally, to you—the reader—thank you.

The fact that you picked up this book tells me you care. You're part of the growing force committed to making work better for people everywhere. I hope this book offers you a few useful tools and much encouragement for the road ahead.

Leadership isn't about getting it right every time. Imperfection is normal—universal, even.

Leadership is about showing up, owning the impact you have, and daring to make it better.

Thank you for daring.

INDEX

M

N

O

ABOUT THE AUTHOR

Jim Brown is the founder of OrgHealth, a boutique consulting firm that equips boards and executive teams to build healthy, high-performing organizations. A trusted advisor to CEOs and directors across North America, Jim brings decades of experience helping leaders turn complexity into clarity and culture into a competitive advantage. In 1995, he cofounded Strive!, later rebranding to reflect a clear and unapologetic purpose: organizational health.

Jim is also the author of the best-selling *The Imperfect Board Member,* a leadership classic that has shaped how thousands of boards think about governance, alignment, and accountability. This new work, *The Imperfect CEO*, continues this journey by inviting senior leaders to embrace imperfection as a pathway to meaningful, transformative leadership.

Jim lives near Toronto with his wife, Karen. Their five adult children and growing circle of young grandchildren fill life with energy, laughter, and love. He's a devoted reader, a fan of yacht rock, and finds joy in long, peaceful walks—especially the kind that invite reflection and fresh perspective.

Earn a Growth Credit for Completing the Coaching Highlights

If you've completed at least 8 exercises from the 10 Coaching Highlights in this book, we want to recognize your effort and help you take the next step.

Visit our website to submit your reflections and choose a growth credit:

OPTION 1	OR	OPTION 2
10% (up to $1,000) credit toward OrgHealth coaching or related services		A discounted Virtual Ascent Team Debrief — a focused 90-minute session to help your team apply the book's insights

Submit at:

OrgHealthTeam.com/imperfect-ceo/growth-credit

What Would It Take to Make Your Board Great?

Boards have enormous influence on company culture, but too often low trust and inefficiencies hold them back.

Jim Brown shares governance stories and tips in a free monthly email for leaders who believe in progress over perfection in the boardroom.

Sign up to receive The Imperfect Board:

OrgHealthTeam.com/email-sign-up